Six Cultures Series: Volume V

The New Englanders
of Orchard Town, U.S.A.

Six Cultures ✳ Studies of Child Rearing Series

Editor:
 Beatrice B. Whiting, *Harvard University*

Senior Investigators
 Irwin L. Child, *Yale University*
 William W. Lambert, *Cornell University*
 John W. M. Whiting, *Harvard University*

Six Cultures Series ❧ Volume V

The New Englanders of Orchard Town, U.S.A.

John L. Fischer
Ann Fischer

John Wiley and Sons, Inc.
New York · London · Sydney

Library of Congress Catalog Card Number: 66-18787
Printed in the United States of America

Introduction

The six monographs in this series report research undertaken in 1954 by a group of social scientists from Harvard, Yale, and Cornell universities. In its broadest conception, the research aimed at exploring cross-culturally the relation between different patterns of child rearing and subsequent differences in personality. The overall research was designed to study the degree to which the experiences of a child in the first years of life determine his behavior and in adult life influence his perception of the world, his philosophy, religion, and code of ethics.

Theories of the relationship between specific types of treatment in early childhood and subsequent personality differences have been advanced by psychologists and anthropologists. This project was established with the hope of being able to test some of these hypotheses using material collected in a standard manner in six parts of the world where families have divergent ways of life and theories and methods of training young children.

The intellectual history of this project begins with the work of Margaret Mead, Ruth Benedict, Edward Sapir, Ralph Linton, Abram Kardiner, John Dollard, and other pioneers in the field of culture and personality whose work formed the foundation of this study. To detail the contribution of these pioneers would demand an essay on the entire new discipline that grew out of the integration of anthropological and psychological theory, an undertaking not practical in this introduction. A brief historical summary by John Whiting appears in the preface to Volume I of this series.

Specifically, the impetus for the present study came from the cross-cultural work on socialization done by two of the senior investigators, John W. M. Whiting and Irvin L. Child, while they were colleagues at the Institute of Human Relations at Yale University. The results of this research were published in *Child Training and Personality* (1953). Using theories of disease as measures of adult personality, the authors attempted to test certain psychological theories relating the treatment of the basic behavior systems in infancy and childhood to adult personality characteristics.

The data on the 75 societies used in these studies were taken from published ethnographies which varied greatly in detail and areas of coverage. The dream of the investigators was to send field teams out to get comparable detailed material on 100 societies. As a first step in accomplishing this aim, the present study was planned.

In 1953 the Committee on Social Behavior of the Social Science Research Council sponsored a seminar* and a conference† to discuss cross-cultural work on socialization. As a result, the *Field Manual for the Cross-Cultural Study of Child Rearing* was prepared (Whiting et al., 1953), and Whiting and Child persuaded William W. Lambert of Cornell University to join them in seeking funds to conduct a comparative study of child rearing. A generous grant from the Behavioral Science Division of the Ford Foundation made it possible to carry out these plans. The fieldwork and part of the analysis and writing of five of the six reports in this volume were financed by this grant. Later analysis and editing were supported by a grant from the United States Public Health Service.

Intensive planning for the study was carried on at Cornell, Harvard, and Yale during the following year under the direction of the senior investigators, William W. Lambert, Irvin L. Child, and John W. M. Whiting. As part of the over-all research plan, further cross-cultural studies were undertaken at Cornell, Harvard, and Yale. Irvin Child, with the assistance of Margaret Bacon and Herbert Barry, investigated the consequences of various types of training on nurturance, responsibility, obedience, self-reliance, and achievement using ethnographic accounts for cross-cultural comparison (Bacon, Child, and Barry, 1963; Barry, Bacon, and Child, 1957; Barry, Child, and Bacon, 1959). William Lambert and Leigh Minturn did further cross-cultural work on aggres-

* The contributing members of the seminar were Barbara Chartier Ayers, Hildreth Geertz, George Goethals, Charles Holzinger, Edgar Lowell, Eleanor E. Maccoby, A. Kimball Romney, Richard Salisbury, William Steward, and John W. Thibaut.

† Attending the conference were Robert R. Sears (Chairman), A. L. Baldwin, R. A. Bauer, Irvin L. Child, L. S. Cottrell, Jr., Leon Festinger, J. G. Gewirtz, A. Inkeles, Harry Levin, Gardner Lindzey, Eleanor E. Maccoby, Carson McGuire, G. P. Murdock, B. Paul, John M. Roberts, R. R. Sarbin, Pauline S. Sears, M. Brewster Smith, R. L. Solomon, John W. Thibaut, and John W. M. Whiting.

sion (Lambert, Triandis, and Wolf, 1959; Triandis and Lambert, 1961), and John Whiting worked on measures of guilt and other mechanisms of internalized controls (Burton and Whiting, 1961).

During June and July of 1954, a Social Science Research Council Summer Conference was held at the Laboratory of Human Development at Harvard. All the research personnel, with the aid of David Aberle of Michigan, Alfred Baldwin and James J. Gibson of Cornell, and Robert Sears of Stanford, wrote the *Field Guide for a Study of Socialization in Five Societies.** This guide appears as Volume 1 of the six culture series. It presents in detail the research plan, the hypotheses to be tested, and the research instruments agreed on by the field teams and the senior investigators. The reader should study this volume in order to understand the content and organization of the monographs and the methods employed in data collection. The theoretical background and the intellectual history of the project are presented in the preface by John W. M. Whiting.†

The five original field teams started work in the fall of 1954 and spent from 6 to 14 months in the field. Although the original design of the study called for a sample of societies whose culture had already been studied by ethnologists, the temperament and motivation of young anthropologists were such that they tended to choose groups who are relatively unknown and who, often from some personal reason, appealed to their interests. The actual groups chosen represent a compromise between the advantages of previous coverage and these personal interests, and also provide the great range of differences desired by the project planners.

Thomas and Hatsumi Maretzki chose the village of Taira on the northeast coast of Okinawa, the largest of the Ryukyu Islands in the Pacific. At the time, Thomas Maretzki was an advanced graduate student in the Anthropology Department at Yale University. Hatsumi Maretzki, a graduate of the University of Hawaii, was on the staff of the Gesell Institute Nursery School. Thomas Maretzki is now an associate professor of anthropology at the University of Hawaii.

Leigh Minturn worked with a group of families of the Rājpūt caste in the town of Khalapur in Uttar Pradesh in northern India. Unmarried at the time of the study, she used the facilities of Morris Opler's Cornell field station in Khalapur which then was directed by John Hitchcock, who collaborated with her in the study. Leigh Min-

* Published in mimeographed form by the Laboratory of Human Development, Harvard University, 1954.

† See also, Lambert, W. W., 1960.

turn received her doctorate from the Social Relations Department of Radcliffe College and Harvard University, and was, at the time of the study, a research associate at Cornell University. She is now an associate professor of psychology at the University of Illinois. John Hitchcock received his doctorate in anthropology from Cornell University and is at present an associate professor of anthropology at University of California, Los Angeles.

William and Corinne Nydegger chose a group of Ilocano-speaking families living in hamlets in northern Luzon in the Philippines. At the time of the study, William Nydegger was an advanced graduate student at Cornell University. His wife had done graduate work in anthropology at the University of Wisconsin. William Nydegger is now an associate professor of anthropology at Pennsylvania State University.

A. Kimball and Romaine Romney chose a group of families in the Mixtecan barrio of Santo Domingo in the town of Juxtlahuaca in Oaxaca State, Mexico. At the time of the study, A. Kimball Romney was an advanced graduate student at Harvard University. His wife attended the University of Colorado. A. Kimball Romney is now an associate professor of anthropology at Stanford University.

John and Ann Fischer agreed to take on the task of establishing bench marks for comparison by studying a group of mothers in the United States. They moved into a neighborhood in Orchard Town in New England. John Fischer, who has a doctorate in social relations from Harvard University, was at the time of the study an assistant professor at Harvard and his wife Ann was an advanced graduate student in anthropology. John Fischer is at present a professor of anthropology at Tulane University and his wife is an associate professor of anthropology at the same university. When they undertook the study, the Fischers had just returned from three years in the Caroline Islands in the Pacific where John Fischer had served as district anthropologist and as native affairs officer on the islands of Truk and Ponape in Micronesia. During this time, Ann Fischer was gathering material on child rearing in Truk; on the basis of this work she received her doctorate from Harvard.

In 1955 a sixth team, Robert and Barbara LeVine, left for Kenya, Africa where they studied a group of homesteads in the Kisii Highlands of South Nyanza District. They were financed by a Ford Foundation fellowship and a National Science Foundation predoctoral fellowship. At the time of the study Robert LeVine was an advanced graduate student in the department of social relations at Harvard University. Barbara LeVine was a graduate student of psychology at

Boston University. She subsequently received a doctorate in social psychology from Northwestern University. Now Barbara Lloyd, she is a lecturer in social psychology at the University of Birmingham in England. Robert LeVine is at present an associate professor of anthropology in the Committee on Human Development, University of Chicago.

To help insure comparability of data, a central clearing house was set up at the Laboratory of Human Development under the supervision of Beatrice B. Whiting, a Yale-trained anthropologist who was a research associate at the Laboratory of Human Development at Harvard. Field notes were mailed in periodically and field problems were discussed by correspondence.

The research design, agreed on by all the field teams, was set up to measure as accurately as possible the child-training practices and the hypothesized individual and cultural differences in personality, especially in the areas of aggression, dependency, and the internalization of various mechanisms of behavior control—areas of special theoretical interest to the senior investigators at Cornell, Yale, and Harvard universities, respectively. Previous research had been done in these areas at the Institute of Human Relations at Yale, at the Iowa Child Welfare Station under the direction of Robert Sears, and subsequently at the Laboratory of Human Development at Harvard University. The research conducted at Iowa and Harvard focused on a study of individual differences among groups of mothers and children in Iowa, Massachusetts, and in three different cultural groups in the Southwest (Sears, Whiting, Nowlis, and Sears, 1953; Whiting, Chasdi, Antonovsky, and Ayres, in press).

In designing the field research reported in this volume, an attempt has been made to assess individual as well as cultural differences. This is one of the unique aspects of the design. The hope was to test hypotheses about the relations of child-rearing practices and consequent personality, both intraculturally and cross-culturally. In the first instance, 24 mothers in each society were studied as individuals in their relationship to one of their children, and each of the 24 children (ages 3 to 10) was observed and interviewed in a standard manner in the hope of detecting behavioral and personality differences. (The mother interviews, child interviews, child T.A.T.'s, and the description of the observations of the children used in the study can be found in Chapter 5 of the *Field Guide for the Study of Socialization*.) The cross-cultural measures included material on child-training practices and also religious beliefs, theories of disease, recreational activities, and so on, collected by standard ethnographic techniques. The outlines for studying these are to be found in Chapter 2 of the *Field Guide for the Study of Socialization*.

A word should be said here about the nature of the social unit each field team chose to study. It was decided to choose a group large enough to yield an adequate sample of individual families. For our design this meant that a group of at least 50 families would be needed to draw our sample of 24, since at least half the families would have grown-up children, children under 3, or no children at all. On the other hand, we wanted a group who knew each other and shared beliefs, values, and practices so that it would be possible to use ethnographic techniques in collecting data and in describing certain aspects of the daily life in cultural terms. The techniques used to locate the Primary Social Unit (P.S.U.) are described in detail in the *Field Guide for the Study of Socialization*, Chapter 6.

In Taira, Okinawa, the Maretzkis visited 63 households in the central part of town and recorded the relationships among the occupants and their kin. The census included about 330 individuals, 83 of which were children under the age of 11.

In Khalapur, India, Leigh Minturn gathered census material in 38 courtyards; all were owned by members of the Rājpūt caste who constitute 40% of the total population of 5000. The courtyards are in a neighborhood inhabited exclusively by members of the Rājpūt caste; the area is bounded on two sides by a river and fields and is separated from the rest of the town on the third side by a temple, school, and meeting house and by a street occupied by another caste group, and on the fourth by a patti division line. (Khalapur is divided into seven political units or pattis.)

In Juxtlahuaca, a town of 3600, the Romneys made a census of 31 courtyards in the Mixtecan barrio of Santo Domingo. This section is separated from the rest of the town, which is inhabited by Spanish-speaking ladinos, by a deep barranca. The census of 31 courtyards included 90 children under 11 years of age.

In Orchard Town, population 5000, a census was made of 42 households, most of them on three adjoining streets in North Village, which has a population of 1000 and is one of the three centers of the town. The families participated together in P.T.A., school functions, women's clubs, and church, as well as in local politics. There were 83 children under 11 in the sample.

In the barrio of Tarong, Luzon, it was necessary to make a census of six adjacent hamlets before a sample of 24 children of the right age could be drawn. The barrio encompasses an area of about two square miles of land crosscut by steep ridges and valleys. The hamlets consisted of from 3 to 17 families. The sample was drawn from 58 families who had 76 children under 11 years of age. The genealogical material collected by the Nydeggers indicates that all but six of the 61 families in the barrio were descended from seven families who settled the area around 1860 (Minturn and Lambert, 1964, p. 18).

In Nyansongo, 18 contiguous homesteads were visited. The families in these homesteads all belong to one clan, and neighboring homesteads often belong to the same patrilineage. The census from which the sample was drawn included 208 individuals of whom 92 were children under 11.

In each of the six societies all the families knew each other and associated at certain times during the year and presumably met our criterion of sharing basic cultural values. If I were to judge the societies on the degree of intimacy of the mothers of the total P.S.U., I would rank the families in Taira as most intimate and those in Juxtlahuaca second. In the other societies there is intimacy in subgroups but not in the entire P.S.U. Although the Khalapur families live close to one another, the women are confined to courtyards, and most of their everyday contacts are limited to women in the same block who can be visited by crossing roof tops.

Women in groups of homesteads in Nyansongo are members of cooperative work teams and hence are on intimate terms with one another. There were three such work groups in the sample. The members of each belonged to the same subclan. Hamlet groups in Tarong are very intimate, especially when families face on the same yard. Visiting, kin ties, and a central school all unite the members of the P.S.U.

The Orchard Town mothers seem to be the least intimate in the sample, although they knew one another by name and knew the names of one another's children.

The P.S.U. groups are defined and selected to maximize the homogeneity which is essential for the use of standard ethnographic techniques. In gathering the background material and much of the material on socialization, the field teams used informants and participant observation. In areas that were not covered by standardized instruments, the data presented in the ethnographies is often based on a combination of discussion with from four to eight informants checked by observation of the daily life of the group. All the field teams lived in the communities they studied for the better part of a year or longer. Three of the field teams had children who played with the sample children. All the ethnographers visited the houses daily, participated in community activities, and became socialized in the habits of the group.

For the individual measures, 24 children were selected from the census material sent in by the field teams according to the following criteria: the sample consisted of four sex-age groups, six boys and six girls from 3-to-5 years of age and an equal number from 7-to-10 years of age.* To maximize the independence of cases, no more than one child was selected from each family. The sample mothers were interviewed and the children interviewed and observed in a standard manner for 12 five-minute periods.

Implicit in the research design is a general concept of the relation of personality to culture, which may be presented as follows: the ecology of an area determines the maintenance systems, which include basic economy and the most elementary variables of social structure. In other words, the type of crops grown, the presence or absence of herding, fishing, and so on, depend on the nature of the terrain, the temperature and amount of rainfall, and the location of the area *vis-à-vis* centers of invention and diffusion. These basic conditions partly determine the arrangement of people in space, the type of houses, and household composition. These in turn set the limits for child-rearing practices. The basic innate needs of both children and parents must be met within this framework.

It is obvious that ecology does no more than determine gross limits for the social structure. Within these limits the nature of the composition of households, neighborhoods, and other social groups will lead to variance in child training. Whether or not a grandmother lives in the house, or whether other relatives are close at hand, will influence a mother's behavior toward her child.

We assume that different patterns of child rearing will lead to differences in the personality of children and thus to differences in adult personality. Since personality may only be inferred, the problem of measurement is difficult on both the individual and the cultural levels. Individual children may be given tests of various kinds, interviewed, or observed. On a cultural level, we may analyze the patterning of child or adult behavior, for example, the games and recreational activity, the rituals or ceremonial life, or we may assess beliefs about the supernatural, theories of disease, or popular folk tales in terms of personality dimensions.

---

* The LeVines' sample was aberrant. They studied six sex-age groups consisting of four children each. They included a group 10-to-14 years of age since they wanted to follow the children through initiation. The Romneys' sample of older children was limited to five girls and five boys 7-to-10 years old.

Chart I indicates this conceptual system in a simple manner. To summarize the conceptual background in another way, the researchers viewed ecology, economics, and social and political organization as largely determining the behavior of the agents of child rearing. They viewed child behavior as an index of child personality and saw adult behavior, beliefs, and values as indices of adult personality. The causal relationships implied in this scheme are open to discussion. Such discussions, with the knowledge available at present, ultimately end with a problem similar to that of the priority of the chicken or the egg.

A word should be said about the type of ecology and economy represented in the sample. Five of the six cultures are agricultural. There are no fishing or hunting and gathering economies, nor are there pastoral people. With the exception of Orchard Town, most of the men in the six societies are farmers. In Tarong, Philippines and in Taira, Okinawa, the most important staple crop is wet rice. In Juxtlahuaca, Mexico and in Nyansongo, Kenya, corn is the important staple. In the latter, eleusine, a grain, is also important. In Khalapur, wheat and other grains are the main food crops.

Chart I   The Relation of Personality to Culture

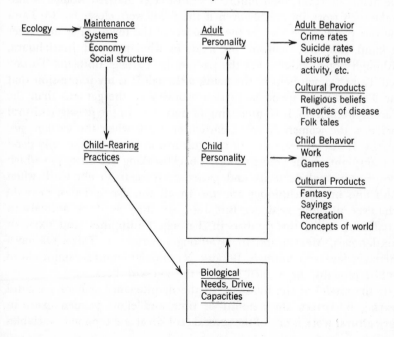

The ecology of the areas, however, makes the farming techniques different: in Taira and Tarong, men and women work together in the fields; in Khalapur and Juxtlahuaca only men work in the fields; in Nyansongo, with the exception of ploughing and building fences, all the agricultural work is done by women. An important variable in determining the amount of agricultural work women do is the distance of the gardens and fields from the dwellings. The gardens are closest in Nyansongo and Tarong, furthest away in Juxtlahuaca and Khalapur. Every Nyansongo woman has gardens close to her house, and she and a group of women who are members of her cooperative work group are responsible for all the gardening. In Tarong the fields and paddies lie directly below the houses which are built on the ridges. The town Juxtlahuaca is situated in a long, narrow river valley. Most of the cornfields near the town and in the valley belong to the ladinos in the Mexican part of town. The Mixtecans' main fields are usually a half-hour walk from home on the slopes of the mountains which follow the river valley. Women do not work in the fields in Juxtlahuaca. Clearing the mountain gardens is done by cutting the trees and undergrowth and burning it off, a technique called slash and burn agriculture. Khalapur is surrounded by fields that are a 15-to-20-minute walk from the courtyards. As in Juxtlahuaca, the Rājpūt women do not work in the fields; however, their enforced seclusion as married women would make such work impossible even if the fields were closer by. In Taira the rice paddies are also on the outskirts of the town. They are closer at hand, however, than are the fields in Khalapur and Juxtlahuaca, although not so close as are the paddies in Tarong. Both the Tarong and Taira women help in the fields, although it is my impression that the Taira women spend more time working in the gardens than the Tarong women do. It is interesting to note that, in the five agricultural societies, the women do more gardening work when the gardens are nearby. It also appears that in rice cultures women are especially good at transplanting the young shoots, a backbreaking and fussy job which requires manual dexterity and patience. Women do not work when slash and burn techniques are use. In all the five societies, men do whatever plowing is done. Buffaloes are used as draft animals in Khalapur, India, the carabao in Tarong, Philippines, and oxen in Juxtlahuaca, Mexico and in Nyansongo, Africa. In Taira, Okinawa there are few large animals. Because Nyansongo families cannot afford to hire ploughs, the women prepare the soil with hoes.

If the model of the influence of the maintenance systems on child rearing is correct, the amount of time and effort women exert in agricultural work is one of the several ecological and economic variables which influence their child-training techniques. The amount of time the fathers spend in the agricultural work and the distance of the fields from the house will influence the amount of time men spend around the house and the amount of time the children see them.

The majority of the families in Nyansongo in Kenya, in Tarong in the Philippines, and in Khalapur, India have large animals which must be watered and pastured. There are no adequate fences in any of these three societies, so humans must see that the cattle do not get into crops. This is done either by tethering the animals, the technique employed by the Tarongans, or by employing a herd boy when the cows are in pasture, the technique used by the Nyansongo and by the Rājpūts of Khalapur. The latter keep the cattle in pens adjoining the courtyards for much of the day and bring fodder into town. The Nyansongo shut the cattle up only at night. During the day, young boys or occasionally younger girls tend the herds. Where the herding technique is used, children are important in the economy and their negligence may ruin the crops essential for the food supply. As a consequence, training in responsibility is early and irresponsibility is severely punished.* Although there are sheep, goats, and burros in Juxtlahuaca, only a few of the families in the sample owned these animals. Here also herdboys are used.

Besides doing whatever agricultural work is expected, some of the women are involved in other economic pursuits. Most of the sample mothers in Taira helped their husbands in lumbering, carrying faggots down from the mountains and bundling them for sale. Some of the Juxtlahuacan mothers cooked for the markets. Some of the Tarongan and Nyansongo women occasionally sold surplus vegetables in the markets. In Orchard Town some women worked outside the home at wage-earning jobs. Only the Rājpūt women had no possible way of earning money.

In sum, the amount of work, excluding child care and housework, required of women varies with the economy and ecology. The Nyansongo women have the heaviest work load, the Orchard Town and Rājpūt mothers the lightest. The Taira and Tarong women seem to rank second and third in economic work load, the Juxtlahuaca fourth. The burden of housework and child care also varies. Here comparisons are difficult, and there are several factors that should be considered. Technological development in the processing of food and in the procurement of water and fuel is one of the determinants of the number

* See Barry, Child, and Bacon, 1959 for a discussion of responsibility training in economies having large animals. The authors interpret the relationship in terms of the amount of property accumulated and owned by members of a society.

of hours a woman spends in cooking and cleaning. For example, the women in Tarong, Philippines, must pound their own rice whereas the women in Taira take theirs to a mill to be processed. Both the Rājpūt women of Khalapur and the Juxtlahuacan women spend long hours preparing grain for cooking. The Orchard Town mother certainly has the easiest lot in this domain; furthermore, she alone has water and fuel readily available in her kitchen.

A second factor that must be considered is the availability of help. As will be described later, in the kin-based hamlet groups in Tarong, Philippines, in the extended family courtyards in Juxtlahuaca, Mexico, and in Khalapur, India, and in the stem family households in Taira, Okinawa, other adult women are available to help with the daily routine of living. In the Nyansongo homestead, there may be co-wives and mothers-in-law within shouting distance. It should be noted, however, that the degree to which women help each other when they live close by and are related varies. In our sample, the closest cooperation between women occurs in Tarong, Philippines; here the kin group is often bilateral and a woman has her own relatives as well as her husband's close at hand. Similarly, in Juxtlahuaca a woman may have her own relatives nearby to help. Affinal relatives seem to be less predictably helpful. In Khalapur the mothers report that they receive little or no help from their sisters- and mothers-in-law, although these relatives are at hand in emergencies.*

In Nyansongo homesteads the cooperation between co-wives varies with the personality, with the difference in age of the wives, and with the executive ability of the husband. It appears that when the second wife is considerably younger than the senior wife, there is more likely to be cooperation. Most Nyansongo mothers, however, use children, usually siblings or cousins, between the ages of 5 and 8 to take over the care of their infants, and these children are the constant companions of their little charges until they can walk and travel with the rest of the children. The Taira mother who is lucky enough to have a mother-in-law or her own mother living in the house receives help with the daily care of her infant. The Orchard Town mother, in contrast to the mothers in the other five societies, has the least help. She can hire baby-sitters, but in general she seldom does so. Even when her own mother or her husband's mother lives in the same town, or even next door, she is not in the habit of asking them to do more than occasional baby-sitting.

---

* It should be noted that the Rājpūt mothers have outside help from sweepers, washers, and water carriers who do some of the daily housework.

Even in child care, however, it should be noted that technological development is important. In our sample, for example, only the Orchard Town mother has a baby carriage. In all the other societies infants must be carried, and children are used in lieu of carriages. Similarly, there are no playpens or high chairs to confine the infant safely while the mother works.

Still a further dimension of comparison is the degree of loneliness of mothers. It is here that the Orchard Town mother is unique: she spends most of her day in the company of her children, isolated from other adults. This is especially true in winter, when it is an effort to bundle up the family and go on a visit.

Associated with loneliness is boredom, and here the Orchard Town mother is similar to the Rājpūt mother in Khalapur who is confined to the courtyard day after day. Both enjoy seeing and talking to someone new and look forward to any breaks in the monotony of the daily routine. Although the Rājpūt mothers usually have adult companionship, they cannot wander downtown or break the monotony either by watching people interact on television or by reading about them in books.

As suggested earlier, the climate influences daily living routine and arrangements in many ways. Children react to excessive heat and cold and grow restive if continuous rains confine them to the dwelling. In all the societies there are days when the temperature is uncomfortably cool (see Chart II). During November through March children may feel cold in the early morning in Juxtlahuaca, Mexico. In June, July, August, and September the nights may be uncomfortably cool in Nyansongo, Kenya. In both of these societies and in Khalapur, India, winter nights probably seem colder than they actually are because of the diurnal variation which averages over 25 degrees. Orchard Town, U.S.A., has by far the most prolonged period of cold and the most days with temperatures that drop below freezing. However, it has insulated buildings and central heating; the children have special winter clothes and hence probably suffer less from the cold than any of the other children in the sample. On the other hand, the Orchard Town mother has to struggle with snowsuits and boots and would often rather stay home than face the task of dressing and undressing children and walking or driving through the snow and ice. She is afraid to leave her children at home alone, even for short periods of time, lest faulty heating equipment set fire to the house. During the winter months the radio broadcasts almost daily the names of small children who have burned to death in their homes. The seasonal contrast in the routine of living is greater in Orchard Town than in any of the other societies.

Chart II Climatic Conditions for the Six Societies[a]

SOCIETY	NYANSONGO	JUXTLA-HUACA	KHALAPUR	ORCHARD TOWN	TARONG	TAIRA
Weather Station	Eldoret	Mexico City	New Delhi	Boston	Aparri	Naha
Observed Period	1930–1945	not given	1866–1943	1870–1949	1928–1937	1891–1935
Temperature						
Hottest month	March	April	June	July	April	July
Absolute high	85°	90°	115°	104°	101°	96°
Daily Range	79–50°	77–51°	102–83°	80–63°	90–73°	89–77°
Coldest month	December	January	January	February	December	February
Absolute low	37°	27°	31°	−18°	59°	41°
Daily Range	76–49°	66–42°	70–44°	37–21°	81–70°	67–55°
Precipitation						
Average yearly fall	40.5 in.	29.4 in.	25.2 in.	40.8 in.	89.5 in.	82.8 in.
Number of months with more than 14 days of rain	3	5	0	0	3	0
Number of months with fewer than 7 days of rain	5	4	10	0	2	0

[a] The material for this table is taken from a report of the Meteorological Office of the British Air Ministry, 1960. The weather stations with the nearest latitude and altitude to the field site were selected.

The sharpest contrast in the weather occurs in Khalapur, where the long periods of heat and drought make the rains in June, July, and August dramatic. Although the actual number of rainy days, even during these months is few (average eight days), the winds that accompany the rains and the intense heat which precedes them in April and May make the seasonal variation striking.

In the other societies it rains frequently throughout the year. But a rainy day ordinarily confines children to their houses only in Orchard Town where precipitation during two-thirds of the year may be accompanied by cold weather. Orchard Town children tend to associate rain with being forced to stay indoors. The rainy season in Juxtlahuaca, which lasts from June through September, can be cold and unpleasant. It rains over 20 days in each of these months and 27 days in two of them (July and August), and the temperature during the same period often falls below 50 degrees. The rainfall, however, is usually a drizzle and does not seem to upset the daily routine so much as the infrequent downpours in Khalapur.

Ecology and economy affect the life of children and their parents in another important way—they partly determine the arrangement of dwellings. The number of people who live in a household, the number of generations which interact daily, the distance between households, and the nature and amount of shared work and play space are factors that influence both the training of a child and his daily experiences.

Chart III shows the composition of households in the six societies. It can be seen that half of the households in Taira, Okinawa include at least one grandparent. It is customary for one son, preferably the oldest, to stay on after his marriage to care for his parents. In Khalapur, India, the majority of the households consist of a man and a woman and their married sons and children or married brothers and their children. In Nyansongo, Kenya, half of the men are polygynists and their wives have separate huts.

Chart III also indicates the average number of adult males, females, and children per household, the extended courtyards in Khalapur having the most people, Orchard Town the fewest. Note that the houses in Nyansongo may have only a woman if her husband is a polygynist who rotates between the huts of his wives. The households have, however, on an average as many children as the extended families in Khalapur. In sum, Nyansongo women have more children than any of the other women in the sample.

Chart IV gives the frequency of the groups whose houses face on an area which the occupants use in common. For the Nyansongo it indicates the people who share a homestead (the people included in these

Chart III Household Composition

	TAIRA	TARONG	KHALAPUR	JUXTLAHUACA	ORCHARD TOWN	NYANSONGO
Nuclear Husband, wife and child. May include siblings of husband or wife	11	19	8	18	23	6
Stem Nuclear family plus 1 or 2 parents of husband or wife	12	3	3	3	4	0
Stem plus Married Brother or married cousins. May include parents' siblings	0	0	7	0	0	0
Extended Lineal Nuclear family plus married children and/or married brothers and/or cousins and their children	1	2	6	0	0	0
Polygynous One wife and her children per house	0	0	0	0	0	8
Other	0	0	0	1	0	2
Average number of adult males	1.3	1.4	2.6	1.3	1.0	.87
Average number of adult females	1.8	1.7	2.4	1.2	1.0	1.0
Average number of children	3.5	3.5	5.7	4.0	2.8	5.8

Chart IV *Courtyard Composition of Groups Larger than the Household Sharing Intimate Space*

	TAIRA	TARONG	KHALAPUR	JUXTLAHUACA	ORCHARD TOWN	NYANSONGO
Households Do not share a yard with another household	23	5	21	5	21	4[a]
Stem Share a yard with one or both parents of husband or wife (who have their own house)	1	3	0	3	3	0
Extended Share a yard with parents of husband or wife and/or aunt or uncle plus married brothers and/or sisters and/or married cousins of husband or wife	0	12	0	6	0	1
Collateral Share a yard with brothers and/or sisters of husband or wife	0	3	0	6	0	0
Collateral Extended Share a yard with married brothers and/or sisters and married children and/or married nephews and nieces of husband and/or wife	0	0	3[b]	2	0	0
Non-kin Share a yard with non-kin	0	1	0	0	0	0
Polygynous Co-wives share a yard	0	0	0	0	0	6
Extended Polygynous Share a yard with married brothers of husband plus husband's parents and/or husband's mothers co-wives and married half brothers	0	0	0	0	0	5
Average number of adult males	1.4	3.2	2.9	2.9	1.1	2.1
Average number of adult females	1.8	4.3	2.6	3.0	1.2	3.2
Average number of children	3.9	7.9	5.9	6.7	2.8	7.1
Total	7.1	15.4	11.4	12.6	5.1	12.4

[a] Includes one polygynous homestead where huts of two wives are far apart and there is tension between the wives.
[b] Includes married first cousins and their children.

units interact daily in an intimate fashion). In Juxtlahuaca the houses face on a private courtyard; in Tarong they surround a yard. Tarong has the greatest number of people who interact on this level of intimacy, and Juxtlahuaca and Nyansongo units are similar in size. Taira and Orchard Town have, on an average, two fewer adults per unit.

As mentioned earlier, the household and dwelling units partly determine the amount of adult help a mother has in raising her children. Our theoretical paradigm suggests, then, that the combined factors of a mother's economic role and the people with whom she lives influence her patterns of child rearing. The first test of hypotheses related to this paradigm are presented in *Mothers of Six Cultures* by Leigh Minturn and William Lambert (1964). Further tests of the hypotheses will appear in a forthcoming volume on the behavior of the children.

The salience of the father in infancy and childhood is another variable that affects the personality development of the society. For a discussion of the relative salience of the father and hypothesized consequent effects on aggressive behavior, see Beatrice Whiting's "Sex Identity and Crimes of Violence: a Comparative study."

Six of the volumes in this series are monographs of each of the six societies. The outline for each is organized around the conceptual system just presented. There are two main parts: one, a description of the adult world into which the child is born—*the ethnographic background*; the second, an account of how the child is trained—*child training*. In Part I, each account starts with a description of the environment and the local setting, including the village plan, the houses, and their interior arrangements. Then the daily routine of living and the economic pursuits of men and women are described. A chapter on social structure follows. In other words, these chapters describe the maintenance system that set the stage for child rearing. The selection of material for the remainder of Part I is also theoretically determined and includes descriptions of either adult behavior or the cultural products that seem to be the best indices of adult personality.

To explain the selection of behavior and cultural products, we must return to the discussion of the dimensions of personality selected for study by the senior investigators. As noted, the hypotheses to be tested focused on aggression, dependency, and the internalization of various mechanisms of behavior control. William Lambert and the Cornell group, because of previous research, were most interested in aggression, Irvin Child in dependency, and John Whiting and the Laboratory of Human Development in the development of internal controls that have been variously labeled as guilt, conscience, and superego.

It was the conviction of the researchers that the areas of study had to be limited and clearly defined if standardized material was to be collected. Chapter 1 of the *Field Guide for the Study of Socialization* is a description of the "systems" of behavior which were chosen for study and the hypotheses which the investigators hoped to test. Although it is impossible to include a detailed description of the theory in this introduction, it is necessary to present at least a summary of the behavior systems and the nature of the hypotheses.*

The nine behavioral systems include succorance, nurturance, self-reliance, achievement, responsibility, obedience, dominance, sociability, and aggression. In the most general terms, succorance is defined as asking others for help; nurturance, as giving help or emotional support; self-reliance, as doing things for oneself; achievement, as striving to meet internal standards of excellence; responsibility, as performing one's expected role duties; obedience, as attempting to meet the demands of others; dominance, as attempting to change the behavior of others; sociability, as making friendly approaches to other individuals; aggression, as hurting others. It was assumed that each of these systems of behavior would exist in some recognizable form and degree in every society and could best be identified by people's responses to specific universal situations. For example, whether an individual who encountered difficulty asked for help or solved the problem himself would indicate the relative strength of his succorance or, in contrast, his self-reliance. A measure of nurturance would be the frequency of the spontaneous giving of help, the reaction to requests for help, or the perception that others need help.

Returning to the monographs, our descriptions of the adult culture of each society include material which we consider relevant to these nine behavior systems.

A chapter on social control is included in each monograph to give information about the frequency of brawls, fights, crimes, and other conflicts and to describe the techniques which the society has devised either for preventing such conflicts from occurring or for stopping existing conflict. This material gives comparative indices of the expressed aggression of the adults and the existence and type of internalized controls. It will be noted, for example, that the incidence of rape is high in Nyansongo, that litigation is frequent in Khalapur and Nyansongo, and that there are few cases of physical violence in either Taira or Juxtlahuaca.

* For a full discussion of behavior systems see Child (1954).

The chapter on medical practices and theories of disease is included because variations in such belief systems were found to be useful indices of personality in the cross-cultural study by Whiting and Child (1953) and in later studies by Whiting (1959). Similarly, the analysis of man's relation to the supernatural was fruitfully analyzed by Spiro and D'Andrade (1958), Whiting (1959), and Lambert, Triandis, and Wolf (1959). Mourning behavior and death ceremonies have also been studied cross-culturally (Friendly, 1956).

We hoped that an analysis of the use of leisure time might be made along dimensions relevant to the nine behavior systems. The man who prefers to be alone in his spare time would be rated less sociable than one who always seeks the company of others. The amount of teasing or playful wrestling in leisure settings, or even the amount of pleasure derived from cockfights, might be used to rate the degree of preoccupation with aggression. The amount of time spent practicing skills might indicate the need for achievement. Whether or not men seek the company of women, men and women, or only men is of interest in assessing personality. Similarly, we might rate a man's personality in terms of his preference for smoking, eating, talking, drinking, dancing, or playing games. The nature of popular games can be analyzed along lines suggested by Roberts, Bush, and Arth (1957).

Part II of the ethnographies is chronologically organized, beginning with pregnancy and childbirth and continuing through preadolescence. The time required to observe this age span made it impractical to systematically study the lives of the adolescent children. The only exception to this is the monograph on the Nyansongo group in Kenya. The LeVines were especially interested in the effect of initiation ceremonies on the Nyansongo boys and girls. For this reason, they selected three age groups for study: the 3-to-7-year-olds, the 7-to-10-year-olds, and the post-initiation boys and girls. The Nydeggers included a brief chapter on adolescence in their monograph on Tarong. The other field teams did not feel that they had enough knowledge to include such a description.

The age span covered in the individual chapters of the six descriptions of socialization differs; each division is made on the basis of the age groups and the transitions recognized by the members of the society. Thus in Khalapur, India, where socialization is not broken by clearly defined stages, there are only three chapters. In Taira, Okinawa, on the other hand, there are named stages and sharp transitions, and the Maretzkis have followed this pattern in describing socialization. Weaning from the breast and back is an abrupt change in an Okinawan child's life. The transition from kindergarten to school age is also clear and dramatic. Before reaching school age a child is "senseless" according to the mothers and cannot be properly trained.

Within these chapters an attempt has been made to cover the treatment of the nine behavior systems by the parent or parent surrogate and to study the child's response to socialization. Obviously, some of the behavior systems are not relevant in infancy. In general, the early chapters in the socialization section concentrate on the handling of succorance, the mother's early contact with the child, the number of other individuals who share in the early care of the child, and their responsiveness to the demands of the infant. Among the hypotheses advanced in the *Field Guide for the Study of Socialization,* several concern the consequence of indulgence in infancy. As stated: "Indulgence in infancy, a large number of nurturing agents, and mild transition from infantile indulgence into childhood will produce (1) a trustful attitude toward others, (2) general optimism, and (3) sociability." It is also stated that training with respect to succorance will tend to influence sociability.

We hope that, on the basis of the information presented in the chapters on infancy, the reader can compare the degree of indulgence in infancy and the number of nurturing agents. A comparison of weaning from the breast and from complete dependence on caretakers should make it possible to evaluate the severity of the transition. For the consequent measures, we may turn either to the description of the behavior of older children or to the behavior and belief systems of adults. Is it true that the Mixtecan child of Juxtlahuaca is comparatively more friendly and sociable in later life than the Nyansongan? In infancy, the Mixtecan is constantly held or carried close to the mother's body, and she responds relatively quickly to the infant's demands. The Nyansongon child is tended for periods of time by a less consistently responsive 5-to-8-year-old child. In adult life, are Mixtecans more optimistic and trustful than the Nyansongans?

With the onset of weaning, other behavior systems become important. Training for self-reliance and the associated punishment for succorance are universal problems, but the degree to which this new behavior is expected of 3-year-olds varies from one society to another. The Orchard Town 3-year-old is feeding and dressing himself, whereas the Khalapur Rājpūt child of the same age may still be dressed and fed by his mother. Similarly, as mentioned earlier, the abruptness of the shift in expected behavior varies. The handling of aggression against parents, siblings, and peers at this age-level is also a universal problem which all parents and socializers must face. Probably closely associated with this behavior system is training for obedience and respect.

The *Field Guide for the Study of Socialization* contains many hypotheses about the antecedents of aggressive behavior in children and adults and stresses the techniques used by parents in the handling of aggression as well as their behavior as models. Specifically, one hypothesis is that permissiveness on the part of parents for teasing behavior should be reflected in the increase of observable unprovoked aggressive behavior on the part of children and adults. Is it indeed true that the Tarongan child who is "playfully" teased by his parents and other adults from early childhood instigates aggressive behavior more frequently than a Rājpūt child whose parents do not "playfully" tease him?

A second hypothesis concerning the handling of aggression states that children will be less likely to retaliate against aggression if parents and socializing agents punish any expression of anger. Again, the Khalapur Rājpūt child whose mother dislikes all expression of emotion, even excessive joy, and the Mixtecan child of Juxtlahuaca who is taught that he will become sick and die if he eats while he is angry should be less aggressive when provoked than the children of Orchard Town.* It will be noted that a distinction is made between unprovoked and provoked aggression. A further distinction is made for instrumental aggression, when a person tends to select aggressive means for attaining his goals. Comparisons between the handling of aggression in childhood may also be used to explore hypotheses about the conditions that lead to the displacement of aggression to others, the use of fantasy to express anger, or the projection of one's own desires to hurt others. For an understanding of consequent measures, the reader may turn to theories of diseases and the nature of the supernatural. Theory predicts that the societies which punish aggression most severely project their anger into the supernatural world and believe in dangerous and malevolent beings or attribute superhuman evil capacity to humans and believe in sorcery or witchcraft. To date, the best socialization variable for predicting the belief in witches and sorcerers is a combination of polygyny and the severe punishment for sex and aggression (Whiting, 1959). Among our societies, the Nyansongans are the most ridden with belief in superhuman individuals. Their treatment of aggression is therefore of particular interest. It is also of interest to

* For further discussion of the hypotheses regarding aggression, see the *Field Guide for the Study of Socialization*, Chapter 1.

speculate whether there is some relation between the Tarongan parents' treatment of aggression and teasing behavior and their belief in whimsical spirits who must be avoided and not annoyed.

Each monograph on socialization also includes an extended section on techniques used by the socializing agent. Our theory stresses the importance of rewards and punishments for the specific types of acts included in the nine behavioral systems. We are interested in the differential effect of various types of rewards and punishments and the conditions under which they are administered. Rewards may be material, such as food or money, or immaterial, as love and acceptance or praise and prestige. Privileges may also be given as rewards. All types of rewards may be given to commend good behavior or to incite desired behavior. Punishments depend on two types of sanctions, injury or abandonment; these may have as referents several types of agents—parents or authority figures, peers, the self, or supernatural agents.

These rewards and punishments may be given for different reasons. The locus of evaluation may be a specific response of the child, some consequence of his action, or the child himself as a person. In other words, a child may be praised because he does a chore well, because he has helped his mother by doing the chore, or because he is a good boy.

Rewards and punishments may also be intrinsic to the environment. For example, in a terrain where there are delicious wild berries, being able to locate, pick, and eat the berries without aid from adults may reward self-reliance. Herding large animals may reward dominance. Hot, humid weather may discourage physical exertion.

The nature and strength of internal controls—mechanisms which keep an individual from breaking the rules of a society—are thought to be related to techniques and agents of socialization as well as to the strength of a child's identification with both parents (Whiting and Child, 1953; Whiting, 1960; Burton and Whiting, 1961; Bacon, Child, and Barry, 1963). To determine the strength of these internal controls, we hoped to observe the differences in children's behavior in the presence and absence of socializing agents. On a societal level, we predicted that when a boy's identification with the same sex parent is weak, there will be a higher incidence of crime (see B. Whiting, in press).

We expected to find that authority figures would be important sanction agents in the adult culture when there was marked differentiation of authority within the nuclear family, when discipline was carried out by or in the name of the head of the house, and when responsibility and obedience training were emphasized. We expected peers to be important agents when there was little differentiation of authority within the family, when the right of discipline was not stressed, and when self-reliance training was emphasized. If these hypotheses are correct, we would expect consequent differences in the social control systems.

For most of the societies, the age period from 6 to 10 emphasizes responsibility training. A comparison of the chores assigned to boys and girls during this period, of the rewards and punishments for good or bad performance or omission, is an index of the training in this behavior system. The age at which different types of chores are assigned gives a clue to the age at which a society considers a child to have "sense," to be capable of reason, and it indicates the beliefs about the nature of the learning process. It will be observed, for example, that the Khalapur Rājpūts believe that children learn primarily by observing; hence there is little direct instruction. One type of responsibility is training children to care for younger siblings, cousins, and neighbors. This training may start very early, as in Taira and Nyansongo, or may be late and unimportant, as in Orchard Town.

The size and composition of play groups and the attitudes of parents about friendliness are described for each age level. It was hypothesized that sociability would be related both to training in nurturance and to the treatment of succorance, but initial comparisons of children's observed behavior indicate that nurturance is probably more closely related to training for responsibility and dominance than to friendliness.

In planning the research, the senior investigators were also interested in discovering age and sex differences in behavior which might be universal (Barry, Bacon, and Child, 1957). Is it true, in spite of radically different treatment in infancy and early childhood in the six societies, that boys and adult men are always more aggressive physically than girls and women and that girls and women are always more affectionate than men? Are there regularities in behavior that hold across cultures? Does succorance always decrease with age and dominance always increase? We have tested these and other hypotheses using the behavioral measures derived from the systematic observation of the sample children (see *Field Guide for the Study of Socialization*, Chapter 1). The results will be published in the forthcoming volume on the *Behavior of Children in Six Cultures*. Preliminary findings do reveal universal sex-age difference. Although these questions cannot be answered from a comparison of the six societies alone, consistent age and sex differences should be followed up by further research.

Mothers in Six Cultures by Leigh Minturn and William Lambert (1964) presents the first perusal of many of the hypotheses just given.

The authors based their analysis on factor scores derived from ratings made on the mothers' answers to the standard interview on child-training practices (see *Field Guide for the Study of Socialization,* Chapter 5). For example, the mother's economic responsibility outside the house, the amount of help she received in caring for her infants and children, and the number of other adult women and their kin relationship are studied in relation to her use of praise or physical punishment, to her concern with training her children to be responsible and to help with daily chores, and to her attitudes toward her child's expression of aggression toward other children and toward herself. The authors discuss the rank order of the societies on these variables and the rank order correlation between these and other variables. They also consider the effect of ecological and demographic variables on the mother's deviation from the norms of her group.

The reader will be aware that in spite of the research design, the data are not always comparable; in the different areas studied, some monographs have better coverage than others. These variations result not only from the personalities, interests, and training of the field-workers but also from the nature of the culture of the society they chose to study.

Although these monographs concentrate on the material that the researchers felt was theoretically relevant, it is hoped that readers with different conceptual systems and different hypotheses concerning human behavior will find it possible to peruse the data with relevant comparisons in mind. Those who were concerned with the project have developed new insights and new hypotheses. Some of these can be explored, but for many the relevant data are not detailed enough and further studies must be conducted. We believe that the need for further studies is inevitable in the social sciences and that progress comes from being willing to state hypotheses, test them, derive new theories, and plan new research to test these.

We believe that the detailed comparison of six societies is useful for generating hypotheses about human behavior. To test hypotheses adequately, the social scientist must study predicted variation among individuals within societies as well as across a larger sample of societies.

In conclusion, we should like to acknowledge our indebtedness to many people and institutions for their advice and help. The opportunity to do the study was provided by the generous support of the Social Science Research Council and of the Behaviorial Science Division of the Ford Foundation, and by a United States Public Health Grant, M-1096.

Various faculty members at the three universities helped in designing and planning the research. A list of these and other contributors will be found at the beginning of this chapter, but we wish to express special gratitude to Robert R. Sears, Pauline Sears, Eleanor E. Maccoby, and Alfred L. Baldwin, who have continued to give valuable advice to the project.

While in the field, each of the teams was assisted by graduates of local universities and schools who acted not only as interpreters but also as informants and friends. The aid that these students gave was invaluable. We wish to thank Nariyuki Agarie, Gurdeep Jaspal, Simeon Nyaechae, John Okiamba, Felix Ombasa, Laurence Sagini, Sri Shyam Narain Singh, Taurino Singson, Muriel Eva Verbitsky Hunt, and Kiyoshi Yogi.

We are deeply grateful to all the staff and students of the Laboratory of Human Development of Harvard University who read and helped edit the monographs. Marilyn Johnson, Celia Kalberg, Dorothy Tao, and Susan Horton were particularly devoted assistants. We wish to express our appreciation to numerous other people for reading and commenting on some or all the monographs, especially Masanori Higa, Geraldine Kohlenberg, and Morris Opler.

We are especially indebted to the families in Nyansongo, Khalapur, Taira, Juxtlahuaca, Tarong, and Orchard Town, who were not only cooperative informants, but also helpful friends. We hope that the children we studied will become proud members of the adult world into which they were born and that these volumes will contribute to mutual understanding so that they may live in a friendlier world.

BEATRICE B. WHITING

Harvard University
September, 1965

BIBLIOGRAPHY

Air Ministry, Meteorological Office. *Tables of Temperature, Relative Humidity and Precipitation for the World.* London: Her Majesty's Stationery Office, 1960.

Bacon, Margaret K., Child, Irvin L., and Barry, Herbert III. A cross-cultural study of correlates of crime. *Journal of Abnormal and Social Psychology,* 1963, **66**, 291–300.

Barry, Herbert III, Bacon, Margaret K., and Child, Irvin L. A cross-cultural survey of some sex differences in socialization. *Journal of Abnormal and Social Psychology,* 1957, **55**, 327–332.

———, Child, Irvin L., and Bacon, Margaret K. Relation of child training to subsistence economy. *American Anthropologist,* 1959, **61**, 51–63.

Burton, Roger V. and Whiting, John W. M. The absent father and cross-sex identity. *Merrill-Palmer Quarterly,* 1961, **7**, 85–95.

Child, Irvin L. Socialization. In Gardner Lindzey (Ed.), *Handbook of Social Psychology*, vol. II. Cambridge, Mass.: Addison-Wesley, 1954.

Friendly, Joan P. A cross-cultural study of ascetic mourning behavior. Unpublished honors thesis, Radcliffe College, 1956.

Lambert, William W. Interpersonal Behavior. In P. H. Mussen (Ed.), *Handbook of Research Methods in Child Development*, Chapter 20, pp. 854–917. Wiley, New York: 1960.

———, Triandis, Leigh M., and Wolf, Margery. Some correlates of beliefs in the malevolence and benevolence of supernatural beings: a cross-cultural study. *Journal of Abnormal and Social Psychology*, 1959, **58**, 162–169.

Minturn, Leigh, Lambert, William W., et al., *Mothers of Six Cultures: antecedents of child rearing*. New York: Wiley, 1964.

Roberts, John M., Bush, R. R., and Arth, M. Dimensions of mastery in games. Stanford, Calif.: Ford Center for Advanced Study in the Behavioral Sciences, 1957 (mimeographed).

Sears, R. R., Whiting, John W. M., Nowlis, V., and Sears, P. S. Some child-rearing antecedents of aggression and dependency in young children. *Genetic Psychology Monograph*, 1953, **47**, 135–234.

Spiro, Melford E. and D'Andrade, Roy G. A cross-cultural study of some supernatural beliefs. *American Anthropologist*, 1958, **60**, 456–466.

Triandis, L. M. and Lambert, W. W. Sources of frustration and targets of aggression: a cross-cultural study. *Journal of Abnormal and Social Psychology*, 1961, **62**, 3, 640–648.

Whiting, Beatrice B. Sex identity conflict and physical violence: a comparative study. *American Anthropologist*, in press.

Whiting, John W. M. Sorcery, sin and the superego: a cross-cultural study of some mechanisms of social control. In *Nebraska Symposium on Motivation*, pp. 174–195. Lincoln: University of Nebraska Press, 1959.

———, Resource mediation and learning by identification. In I. Iscoe and H. Stevenson (Eds.), *Personality Development in Children*. Austin: University of Texas Press, 1960.

———, and Child, Irvin L. *Child Training and Personality: a cross-cultural study*. New Haven, Conn.: Yale University Press, 1953.

———, Chasdi, Eleanor M., Antonovsky, Helen F., and Ayres, Barbara C. The learning of values. In E. Z. Vogt (Ed.), *The Peoples of Rimrock*, Cambridge, Mass.: Harvard University Press, in press.

———, et al. *Field Manual for the Cross-Cultural Study of Child Rearing*. Social Science Research Council, New York, 1953.

———, et al. *Field Guide for a Study of Socialization*. Six Cultures Series, vol. 1. New York: Wiley, 1966.

About the Authors

In selecting the sample for study we included a group of families in a New England town so that we would have bench marks for comparison. Although it is difficult for "natives" to collect ethnographic data which is comparable to that collected by an individual of a different culture, the account of Orchard Town, presented with a format similar to that of the other ethnographies, will give the reader some idea of how a Rājpūt from Khalapur or an Okinawan from Taira would react to the description of his life.

John and Ann Fischer were assigned the difficult task of conducting the study in a New England community. John Fischer, who has a doctorate in anthropology in social relations at Harvard, and his wife had spent three years in the Caroline Islands in the Pacific where he had served as the district anthropologist on Truk and Ponape and later as a native affairs officer. Ann Fischer had gathered material for a doctoral thesis for the Harvard Anthropology Department on Trukese mothers and their infants. Their two daughters, Nikko and Mary Anne, were born on the islands and spent their early years with Trukese children. We felt, therefore, that the family would have an objectivity about New England which would help them to do a comparable study in their own society. They moved into a community and selected a group of families who were largely members of a Baptist church situated near their house. John Fischer volunteered his services as a Sunday School teacher. The yard of their house, which was large and inviting, was a gathering place for many of the children. The Fischers had by far the hardest job, from one point of view, for their informants quite understandably felt that the Fischers knew the answers to the questions they asked. The mothers were interested in child rearing but more concerned with the particular than the general. The Fischers had difficulty in convincing them that they were not "authorities" and that the project was designed to learn from them rather than to conduct a clinic. Although it was easy to evaluate individual differences, it was difficult to see the large patterns. We have often thought that, unlike the other teams, who had college graduate "native" assistants, the Fischers would have found it profitable if they had had a non-Western European assistant to gather the cultural material.

John Fischer is now a professor of anthropology at Tulane University. Ann Fischer is an associate professor of anthropology at Tulane University (Newcomb College). Recently (1961–1962), the Fischers made a study of children's personality development as influenced by family composition in Japan.

Contents

Part I   Ethnographic Background

Part II   Child Training

Contents

Part I

Ethnographic Background

❋
❋
❋
❋
❋
❋

Chapter 1

The Setting

Before beginning this field study, we were residing in New England while finishing our doctoral work in anthropology. In choosing a community to study, we first defined a general area containing a couple of dozen communities which seemed to be relatively small and stable. We then reconnoitered until we found one meeting the general requirements and with suitable and strategically located living quarters for our year of study. To preserve the anonymity of the people involved, we shall refer to the community involved as North Village and to the officially organized town in which it is located as Orchard Town.

Since Orchard Town was within a reasonable traveling distance of our home at the time, we were able to visit it from time to time before actually moving there. Our initial introduction to the people of Orchard Town came through the then Superintendent of Schools. He had studied at the Harvard Graduate School of Education, with which we were affiliated during our study. Although this superintendent left to take a foreign job shortly after we met him, before leaving he introduced us (at his farewell party) to some of the officials connected with the schools and to other townspeople.

We made no special efforts to give publicity to our study, since we wished to preserve the anonymity of the town and people as far as possible. However, we explained the general purposes of our work without hesitation to anyone who asked, child or adult. In general, we told people that we were studying what it was like to be a child in North Village, that we planned to watch the children doing different things, and to ask people questions, about the children in particular and the community in general as the setting in which the children grew up. In the process of obtaining interviews from the mothers and children, all parents in the 24 families of the sample were necessarily informed that we wished to study one of their children in detail. The only formal publicity the project received in town was a speech given to the local PTA, a flourishing organization, by Beatrice Whiting, after we had been engaged in fieldwork for several months. In this speech she described the general purposes of the project and something about the fieldwork in the other five cultures.

We met more people through the local Protestant church than in any other fashion. All of the families in our sample either had some connection with the church or associated with people connected with the church. The minister, who, incidentally, was taking graduate work in religious psychology, was especially understanding of the purposes of our study and helpful in introducing us to people around town.

Since we were studying our own culture, or a not very unusual variant of it, we were in a different position from most anthropological fieldworkers. As residents, and later registered voters, of the town, we were considered by most people to be as capable of assuming the general duties of citizens as anyone else. There was little difficulty in arranging genuine participation in many aspects of the life of the community. The male ethnographer, for instance, taught Sunday School to a group of fourth-grade boys every Sunday during the school year. The difficulty was rather in trying to maintain free access to opposing groups in the community by avoiding too full participation in some of them. As members of the culture ourselves, we had constantly to check our tendency to choose sides on issues dividing the community, since we also tended to feel that it was proper for us to participate and that we were as qualified as anyone else to pass judgment. Thus not only did people in the community itself tend to think of us as not too exceptional and as equally liable to civic obligations as anyone else, but also we ourselves felt more obliged to participate than we would have in studying a foreign culture.

Unlike fieldworkers in many foreign cultures, we had little entertainment value for members of the town. If anything, our academic background seemed a little dull or stuffy to some of the townspeople.

In studying our own culture we found it difficult to get people to make generalizations about life in the town. Cultural questions would be reinterpreted as questions about individual differences within the culture or they would be airily dismissed with the statement, no doubt often correct, "Oh, you know how it is." A foreign ethnographer would probably have been more successful in getting the people to talk more generally about their community and its life, but on the other hand would probably have been slower to appreciate differences between various people.

We were fortunate in our choice of living quarters. We were able to rent the first floor of a house with a large yard which had the reputation of being a sort of playground for the neighborhood children. The yard had a broad lawn, a sandbox and sandpile, a swing attached to a high tree branch, and other attractions for children. The house faced the North Village green and was located next to the Protestant church. The business block was father down the street beyond the church. A number of the families in our sample lived within easy walking distance of our home, although others lived in newer houses on the outskirts of the village.

Orchard Town was settled and organized as a town in the colonial period, and native residents express pride at the part their ancestors and predecessors played in the Revolutionary War. Through most of its history Orchard Town has been primarily a farming town with some small local factories and craftsmen. After the initial period of settlement, the population has remained rather constant throughout most of its history, but recently, with the suburban expansion of nearby cities, the population has been increasing as city workers have moved in and bought homes. At the same time, with improvements in the nationwide transport of farm products, local farming has suffered by competition with areas favored with better soil and climate and is now much reduced in scope.

There are three major centers of population in Orchard Town, which we label here North Village (the community which we studied), Center Village, and Depot Village. The original center of the town was Center Village, and it is here that the town hall is still located. North Village and Depot Village both grew larger after the railroad was laid through them in the mid-nineteenth century. The railroad bypassed Center Village because of the protests of some of the inhabitants, and Center Village is now somewhat smaller than the other two.

The long-time residents of Orchard Town—and it is these in whom we were especially interested—like to think of the town as rural and as exemplifying the rural New England virtues of friendliness, self-respectability, moderately paced living, conservatism in respect for the law, and freedom from pretentiousness. At the same time, they recognize with mixed feelings that the nature of the community is changing because of the rapid growth produced by immigration from the cities. The increased population has made it impossible to fit all the citizens into the town hall at town meeting, has overcrowded school buildings —even though new ones have been built—and otherwise taxed public facilities. The newcomers, initially at least, tend to be more "liberal" politically and tend to have numerous ideas as to town improvements which appear unnecessary to many long-time residents. Some of the latter lament the passing of the old order and talk about moving farther out, while others welcome the growth and change, though not without nostalgia, as offering new life and opportunities for improvement.

Physically the people of Orchard Town present no apparent differences from a somewhat mixed Old American group elsewhere in the country. In emotional types, also, they greatly resemble the people in other established American groups. Any trends toward differences from Americans in other parts of the country can probably be attributed to regional rather than specifically local differences—to New England versus other parts of the country rather than to Orchard Town versus other nearby towns. Characteristics which seem to help distinguish Orchard Town people, and probably rural and small-town New Englanders generally, from the population of other parts of the country include among others a greater tolerance for personal eccentricity, a somewhat greater interest in the past, a relative lack of ostentation, and often a certain reserve or dignity of manner with strangers. All these characteristics appear to be more marked in the older people than the younger. They are in accord with the popular stereotype of New Englanders but it is our impression that while the people of Orchard Town did fulfill the stereotype to a certain degree, they are basically quite similar in character to small-town people in many parts of the country.

The population of Orchard Town is not very stable and is becoming less so; it is a mobile one. To a certain extent this has perhaps always been true. The first minister of the North Village Protestant church, for instance, resigned to go to California at the time of the 1848 Gold

Rush. The villagers have relatives in far parts of the country. The father of one informant worked on the Panama Canal and that of another visited Samoa as a sailor. Furthermore, many of the present villagers have themselves lived in various parts of the country, and, of course, during World War II, men who joined the Armed Services traveled to distant parts of the world.

A rough idea of the origin of the population can be gained from a sample of 85 parents, composed of one parent for each of 85 children entering the first grade in the year 1953. Usually the parent given is the father, although in some cases if the mother filled out the report, she did so for herself. The children and their parents come from all parts of Orchard Town, not just North Village, but it seems likely that the proportions in the sample would apply about as well to North Village as to the town as a whole. Of this sample, 8 (roughly 10%) were born in Orchard Town; 16 in nearby small towns; 12 in small towns in some part of New England—adding to a total of 36 with some kind of New England, small-town background. Thirty-three more were born in New England cities of varying size, making a total of 69 out of 85 from some part of New England. Four more were born in other eastern states, 5 more were born in far states, 4 were born in Canada, and the remaining 3 were born in Europe—note that 16 out of 85 were *not* born in New England, about one fifth of the population. However, an even smaller ratio are genuine natives of the town; moreover, some of the "natives" in this categorization, that is, people born in Orchard Town itself, were born of foreign parents.

Another thing to note about the population is that it is growing, and it is expected to continue to grow. There has been a very gradual growth in the population ever since the beginning of the town, but the greatest growth has taken place within the last few years, since World War II. Most of the recent growth appears to be accounted for by new people moving into the town. The population of the town as a whole at the time of our study was nearly 5000, of which about 1600 lived in North Village. Population throughout most of the town's history was about half this.

Orchard Town is located on the edge of the commuting area of one of the large New England cities. In addition to North Village, the town includes the two other principal centers of population: the Center, where the town hall is located, and Depot Village, the most important train stop. The description here will be limited mainly to the village studied, North Village. Certain important features and places which are not in any one of the village centers should be noted, however. Two of these are the main highway and the railroad which bisect the town. Another is the town dump, to which most residents of Orchard Town, in whichever village they reside, must pay frequent visits because there is no collecting service for trash. There is also the high school and, adjoining it, a primary school for the first two grades only. This is located roughly midway between the three centers of population. There are also a few small factories which are located between the centers of population.

Legally, Orchard Town is divided into three precincts, the three centers of population corresponding to a precinct. Besides its legal distinctness, North Village has the following attributes of a community· it has a school (for third to sixth grade, at the time of the study); it has a Protestant and Catholic church, a fire house, a small business district, a small green or square, and a railroad station at which some trains stop. Some people use the train for commuting to the city and have for many years, although train service is not as frequent as it used to be when driving was more difficult.

North Village has only about four principal streets. Two of these are state routes and are maintained mostly by the state. Many of the new houses are located on some of the small side streets. The main highway, which is used by commuters to the big city, is located about a mile from the center of North Village. Traffic is heavy and moves fast along the main highway but under rather strict police control on the lesser highways. Traffic is very light on the side streets and moves slowly, for most of the streets are narrow and poorly paved.

The center of North Village (see map 1) contains a small green on which the Protestant church is located. Adjacent to the green and church is a small, block-long business district. The green is quite small, and it is there only because a wealthy local resident gave this plot of ground to the town, within the lifetime of many now living; it is not the sort of large, planned green which is found in many New England towns. Such a green is found in Orchard Town only in Center Village. Originally there was a house on the site of the North Village green. This was torn down to make the green. A cemetery is located on the edge of the village.

The business district contains two grocery stores, one small restaurant, another lunch place with a fountain, a drugstore, a clothing store selling ready-made clothing (especially children's clothing), a materials store selling cloth for clothes and drapes, a barber shop (with one barber), a beauty shop (one beauty operator), a hardware store, and another store, very popular with the children, which sells principally stationery, magazines, newspapers, candy, and toys. There is a small railroad station, which is open for the convenience of passengers

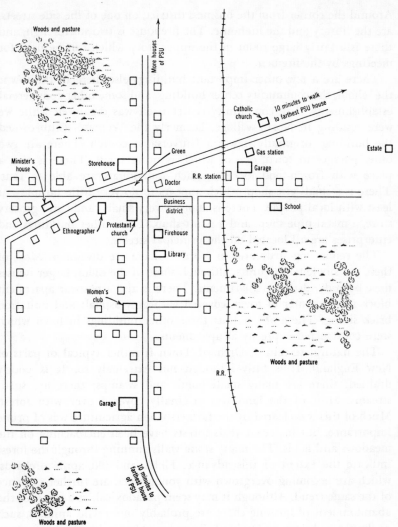

Map 1. Center of North Village.

waiting for trains but which no longer sells tickets. Across the railroad tracks from the rest of the business district there is a gas station, a garage, a trucking company, and a storage place for farm products. On the green there is also a building now used for apple storage, which was formerly the hall of a men's fraternal society. The Catholic church is on the other side of the railroad tracks, opposite the gas station.

Around the corner from the business district, on one of the side streets, are the library and the firehouse. The firehouse is two stories high, and there is a fairly large room in the upper story which can be used for meetings by the firemen.

There are a few other important buildings elsewhere in the town: the school, the community center building, and some other commercial establishments. The community center itself was organized while we were residing in North Village. Formerly the Women's Club owned the building; originally it was a Universalist church. There are two other garages in town, one of which is quite small. There is also a place with frozen-food lockers, which individuals are able to rent. There is a small gift shop, which appears to do very little business, at least with local people. There is another very small candy and grocery store, a metal pipe shop, and a paint shop. These other buildings and enterprises are all located on the principal streets.

The remaining structures in North Village are dwellings. Most of these are single-family units, although some of the older, larger houses have been divided into apartments. There is also a postwar apartment block in the center of town, covered with grey asphalt and imitation brick siding. There are at least three other buildings in town which were constructed expressly as apartments.

The natural terrain of Orchard Town is rather typical of parts of New England. It is hilly although not extremely so. It is poorly drained; there are many small ponds and swamps; there are small streams. Most of the land was originally covered over with forest. Much of this was cleared by the farmers when agriculture was of prime importance, but in recent years forests have been encroaching on the meadows and fields. The many stone walls running through the forest indicate the extent of this advance. Fields and old apple orchards, which are becoming overgrown with young trees, are further evidence of the same trend. Although it may seem paradoxical, as a result of the abandonment of farming there are probably more wild animals, such as skunks and deer, in Orchard Town now than a hundred years ago.

A number of ponds and lakes provide swimming in the summer and skating in the winter. These ponds, together with numerous small streams, offer opportunities for fishing, although, according to old inhabitants, the quality of fishing around Orchard Town has decreased in the last generation because of water pollution. Trout fishermen can easily travel to better fishing grounds in nearby areas.

The woods and fields of Orchard Town offer hunting of game birds and even some deer. The meadows and farms are also valued as places for collecting wild berries, especially bluberries. One of the most popular places for collecting blueberries is at the bog at the town dump. The town dump is located at one side of this bog, and it is being gradually filled in by the refuse which the citizens dispose of there. This is covered over periodically with sand and eventually will form a plot of dry land. Berries are said to be less common now than a generation ago, because cow pastures, which were once a very suitable site for wild berries, have been partially overgrown by shrubs.

The climate of Orchard Town is typical of New England. An inland town, it does not have the moderating effect of the ocean in the summer; summers get rather hot. In winter, temperatures go well below freezing at times, and snow, although not uncommon, seldom covers the ground for more than a few weeks.

The dwelling is one of the cultural features which most sharply distinguishes New England from the other societies described in this volume. It has brick chimneys, doors with hinges, latches, and locks, hardwood floors, woven rugs, upholstered chairs and couches, glass windows which let in the light and keep out the cold, central heating, running hot and cold water, indoor flush toilets, indoor bathtubs and showers, automatic refrigeration, gas or electric stoves, telephone, radio, television, basements, second stories, and attics. The New England house shares with that of other societies the separation of the dwelling into rooms which are used for different functions, such as cooking, sleeping, eating, and entertaining.

Although two of the families in the sample lived in apartment houses, the rest were divided about equally between old New England two-story houses and modern single-story houses. (See Figure 1 for plan of typical house and yard.) The former were larger and more costly to maintain. In addition to kitchen, bathrooms, bedrooms, and living rooms, these old houses were likely to have parlors, pantries, studies, and attics. The basements of these old houses were more likely to have been root cellars which were modified when the furnace was installed and therefore seldom used as a play area for the children or for television as is the case with the basements in the modern house. The outbuildings associated with the old houses are more likely to be barns than garages. Finally, large shade trees are likely to surround the old houses, making them cooler in summer.

The kitchen is probably the most important room in the New England house. Nearly all the families in our sample have a kitchen which contains a gas or electric stove, a refrigerator, an electric washing machine, and a sink with running hot and cold water. Around the walls are dressers, cupboards, and shelves for the storage of cooking and eating utensils. In addition, most of the kitchens contain a table and

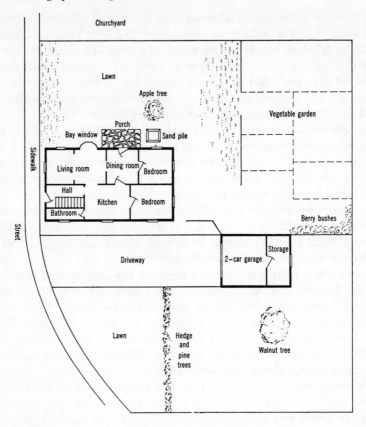

Figure 1. Plan of typical house showing ground floor and yard.

chairs at which most family meals are eaten, the dining room or dining-living space being used only for formal dinner parties. Since cooking, eating, and washing all occur in the kitchen, this is the center of family life during the daytime. In the evenings after supper this center generally moves to the living room or to the TV room.

The New Englander's inability to throw anything away, for "it might come in handy sometime," puts a strain on the house and outbuildings. The attic is generally filled with materials of little practical use. Similarly, every available bit of extra space in the basement, closets, garage, or barn is crammed with broken furniture which might some day be repaired, old clothes sometimes used by the children for "dressing up," baby carriages, "which will be perfectly good for the grandchildren," and the like. Sometimes extra buildings or additions are built just to provide more storage space.

Most of the houses are surrounded by large yards, many of which contain swings and sandpiles. Flower beds and decorative bushes are generally to be seen on the street side of the yard and fruit orchards, berry patches, and vegetable gardens in the backyard.

The above description of house and yard applies to Orchard Town people for most of the year, but most of the North Village families in our sample also spend some time in the summer at a "camp." The stay at the camp serves as an annual period of relaxation from the restrictions at the house and from the stimulation of television or other mass media. A *real* camp was defined as surrounded by forest, no electricity, no plumbing, no television or radio, and with the nearest road a half mile away. Some of the camps are within a few miles of Orchard Town and within commuting distance of home. Others are as far as a day's drive away. In any case, the camps seem to be very isolated and in a place with different neighbors. Living conditions at camp are quite different from those at home, and the children as well as the rest of the family look forward to their annual stay there.

❧
❧
❧

Chapter 2

Basic Economy

Most of the economic activities which take place inside Orchard Town are services or are concerned with the distribution of products. There are a few small factories in town, but the specialization and centralization of industry have largely taken labor out of Orchard Town and into bigger neighboring communities. This process has increased with the years and has slowly changed the basic economy from an original farming community supplying many of its own needs to one dependent on its integration with the economy of the nation.

Only two of the fathers in our sample are self-employed. One runs a chicken farm, and the other is a consultant. The remainder are all salaried employees or wage earners. Many of the occupations would fall in the category of skilled labor, but the range is from truck drivers to bankers. The sample is just about evenly split between white-collar and blue-collar jobs.

Nearly all the men commuted to their work, some of them going to the metropolitan area each day. The fathers therefore are seldom present for the noonday meal except on weekends.

The basic economy of Orchard Town, like the economy of much of the nation, is remarkably stable throughout the seasons. Man-made rest periods cause much more variation in the scheduling of the basic economy than the climate or the seasonal round. Every week the basic economy slows down for Saturday and Sunday. It also slows down for national holidays.

There is some seasonal difference in that men's work slackens during the summer. Stores are closed on Wednesday afternoons, and many men take summer vacations a few weeks during the summer or they may take longer weekends during the summer. Summer is to a certain extent the time for consumption of the winter savings.

Another variation in the summer is that some families do supplementary vegetable gardening. In former days women used to can their own vegetables, but they do not do this as much now. Some seasonal foods are preserved, especially delicacies such as strawberries and blueberries, which though available at other seasons in the stores, would be more expensive than one would wish to pay. At present, roughly the same food is available all year in the stores, since it is shipped in from far parts of the country.

The basic necessities of life as well as many of the amenities are distributed adequately throughout the population of Orchard Town. There is practically no real danger of famine or food shortage or lack of housing or clothing or other lack in the basic economy, although most of the inhabitants have a desire for more luxurious food, better-looking clothes, bigger houses, bigger TV sets, better cars, and the like. There are a number of restrictions on the consumption of food by the children, but these restrictions are not based on the danger of shortage of food. Children do not have to worry about being inadequately clothed in terms of protection from the weather, although they may be concerned about whether their clothes look as well as other children's.

Old people who lack savings are in a difficult economic position, but they receive government aid if necessary. Even they have no serious lack of the basic requirements of food, clothing, and shelter.

A few people in the town have a relatively low standard of living, since they have to live on money from relief funds. Most of these, however, are old people who do not live in households with children. Our sample, therefore, contains none of these people. Most of the families in the sample live on an income which does not allow any savings to be made beyond payments on a home mortgage and insurance payments. Perhaps 6 families in the 24 would be an exception to this rule. On the other hand, probably none of the 24 families could be said to be in debt, beyond the amount of the mortgage on their homes. Some families do a very small amount of installment buying.

Most of the wealth which is consumed is distributed throughout the population through the medium of entrepreneurs. Most goods are acquired by purchase through known entrepreneurs, and therefore shopping is an important activity. Women do most of the shopping. They must buy food regularly, and they use these trips to the store for food to do other forms of shopping as well. Practically all families in town have a car of some sort, and the women use it at certain times at least to go shopping. Usually the women themselves drive. If they do not, the husbands drive them shopping on weekends or evenings when the stores are open. There is no regular means of transportation except for the privately owned car and occasional trains which take passengers into the city. Most people rarely buy anything from a distance as far away as the city. Shopping for large quantities is usually done in nearby towns; for small quantities it is done in North Village.

The largest share of the family income is spent on goods which are immediately or almost immediately consumable—food and clothing. Although food is mainly purchased at the stores, door-to-door vendors are another source of food. Milk, eggs, bakery products, a little fish, and a few vegetables are sold this way. Home-grown vegetables and poultry supply some needs. Facilities for food storage are good. Canned and dried foods can be stored indefinitely in cupboards, and perishable food is stored in the refrigerator. Some families have locker space in the freezer plant where they can store other perishable foods for a long period. Many foods can be purchased already prepared for consumption.

There is not much food available in the fields or in the yards, but what little there is is not strongly prohibited to children. Children would be advised not to pick fruit belonging to other people, but it is not felt very serious for children to take these for their own consumption in season. It would be more serious for children to take vegetables from the vegetable gardens, but they would feel less desire to do this. Children are supposed to get most of their food at meal-times, but they are allowed some sweets and fruits in between meals and are also given small sums of money which they use mostly to purchase gum and candy. A child's between-meal food, or the money for it, may come either from his own home or from his friends.

Houses are very permanent. If preserved from fire, they last almost indefinitely. There are houses in town which are probably two centuries old. Although houses need periodic repairs, they do not fall down and are rarely torn down. The most common way to get a house is to buy one. Some families in our sample had inherited their houses. Recently many new houses have been built.

Within the nuclear family, labor is divided between adults and children and between men and women. The division of labor by generation can usually be dismissed simply by saying that the adults do most of the labor and the children do very little. Children used to do more and in some conservative families still do a significant amount of work around the home, but compared with other cultures the children of Orchard Town do not do very much.

The economic function of the men of the family is to provide the greater part of the cash and also to take care of repairs around the house and sometimes even to construct the house. Four fathers in the sample of 24 had largely built their own homes. The woman's function is to do routine housework, purchase food, and prepare it. It is considered desirable to have a variety of foods for the evening meal, and this increases the time spent in food preparation. Most women have sewing machines and make some articles of clothing for themselves and their children. Many of them also spend some time mending and knitting. These activities are not considered as important as cleaning the house and preparing the food. Women are also responsible for laundering the clothes and for cleaning and decorating the house. Many of the women have jobs or ways of earning supplemental cash. Some of the ways in which the women in our sample supplied extra cash for the family were: baby-sitting, running a nursery school, giving riding lessons, dressmaking, and serving as secretarial help for their husbands.

Occupational specialization among the men is great and has increased considerably in the last few generations as the economy of Orchard Town has been integrated with the national economy. Of a group of neighbors, each man usually has a different occupation or works in a different place away from contact with his neighbors.

In contrast to earlier days, there is a greater tendency for the men to be employed in fairly large organizations. There have been workshops or small factories in Orchard Town for generations, but the older establishments were mostly smaller ones.

In contrast to farming and small, locally unique business enterprises, most modern jobs demand that the individual get along with people, that he be on the good side of the customers or on the good side of the boss. One resident told a local small businessman jokingly, "You are just as ornery underneath as I am, my friend, but you don't exude it as we do; you are too afraid of losing that dollar, and you're right, you'd lose it too. There's lots of people would stop coming to you if they got angry at you."

Most people think of a job primarily as a means of getting cash. However, there is a concern, varying with individuals, for doing something or having some kind of job that is of service to others. Professional people, such as teachers, doctors, ministers, and lawyers, tend to express this concern or to obtain a certain amount of credit for it from other people.

✣
✣
✣

Chapter 3

Kinship and Marriage

As has been shown in many studies of American culture, kinship is not very important in regulating human relations outside of the nuclear family. This is true because there is little interaction with other relatives. The nuclear family is formed by marriage and ideally produces children. The husband, wife, and their children generally live in a separate dwelling unit. Widowed parents of the husband or wife are possible additions to the household, although such additions are regarded with distaste by most people. In our sample only one such instance was noted out of 24 families—a widowed mother's mother. An unmarried mother's sister provided another case of an added member to the household.

Although there were no cases of the extended family household that was so common in New England during colonial days, there were several cases in which grandparents lived in an apartment attached to the house of one of their children. There were three cases of such an arrangement in our sample. In two cases the daughter was involved and in the other the son.

There seems to be some tendency for couples to reside in the wife's community if the husband's occupation permits this. Transportation is efficient enough for men to commute from some distance. Living in the locality where the wife has friends or relatives is much preferable, since the woman spends most of her day in or near the home. Five of the families of our sample exhibited this matrilocal residential pattern, whereas by contrast only one family was patrilocal, that is, the father born in Orchard Town and the mother from away. In 3 of the families, both parents were brought up in Orchard Town. In the remaining 15 families, both parents were brought up elsewhere, usually somewhere in New England so that grandparents if still living could be visited by a drive of a few hours at most. In only two families did both parents come from outside New England, and even in one of these the maternal grandparents had moved to a nearby town.

Within the nuclear family all children are legally equal. They are supposed to inherit equally and should be treated equally. One informant noted that another family in trying to achieve this equality of children had slighted the more competent child in an effort to raise a less competent child to equality.

Marriage is monogamous and for life. It is in no sense a contract between the two families but rather a contract between the two individuals involved—the well-known contract to love, honor and obey and cleave only unto this spouse so long as they both live. A divorced woman may take her children, if any, and return to live with her parents, however. One divorced woman and her two daughters were living with her parents, an arrangement which allowed the woman to work for the support of her children. Often, however, the child who has left to marry and then returns to his family finds his place in the family is not as it used to be and leaves to live alone or with friends. There were a few divorced and remarried individuals in the community. None of these were included in our sample. The general sentiment is against divorce.

All marriages are not considered equally preferable. Preferred marriages are those between persons of near equal age and status. There is some sentiment against marriage between persons of different religion or race. There is some intermarriage between Protestants and Catholics involving Catholics of both Irish and Italian background.

These latter mostly came from a nearby town. Little other inter-marriage occurs partly because there are few representatives of other races or religions in or near Orchard Town.

Adoption is a very rare phenomenon in North Village. It happened once during our year of residence, and no other cases were recorded by us. Legal adoption, however, is such a long and difficult process that it is only undertaken by those who are truly desperate to have children.

The kin terms for mother, father, grandmother, grandfather, uncle, and aunt, either in their formal or familiar (mother or mom) terms, are used in address to indicate respect. Paternal or maternal grand-parents are distinguished by coupling the appropriate surname with a kin term, for example, Grandpa Jones, whereas uncles and aunts are particularized by coupling the given name with the kin term, for example, Uncle George. First and second cousins are generally recog-nized as kin, but beyond this they are recognized only as being a distant relative, and personal compatibility is more important than kinship in determining their relationships. One man used the term "barnyard relation" for a remote cousin living in the vicinity. One high school girl whose family are long-time residents in the town said, "I'm related to everybody, not first cousins or anything."

Kinship terms usually applied to blood relatives are sometimes ex-tended to affinals. This is particularly true of the uncles and aunts of one's spouse. Parents-in-law are also sometimes referred to as "mother" and "father" with surnames sometimes added. In other cases first names are used, and still others manage to avoid addressing their parents-in-law at all.

✤
✤
✤

Chapter 4

Social Organization

To a certain extent people living in adjacent houses form neighbor groups regardless of status differences. Neighbors would speak to each other on the streets and, especially in the warmer parts of the year, might talk with each other in their yards. There are also informal friendship groups among the women who visit each other during the day and talk to each other on the telephone. These are not identical with the local neighbor groups although they may include neighbors. The attitudes toward neighbors are summarized in the statement of one woman: "The old ladies are good neighbors; they are quiet."

There are a number of voluntary associations and clubs in Orchard Town and in North Village. Those connected with the church are described more fully, in connection with religion; the PTA (Parent-Teacher Association) is described in connection with education; economic organizations are described in connection with basic economy. The remainder considered here are more concerned with recreation or civic improvement. More prominent associations include the American Legion, Veterans of Foreign Wars, Masons, the Odd Fellows, Voluntary Fire Department, bowling teams, Sportsmen's Club, the Community Center, the Eastern Star (which is the Women's Auxiliary of the Masons), the Women's Club, the Garden Club, the Hospital Auxiliary. There are also local people who canvass for contributions for the Red Cross and for the United Community Service or the Red Feather Campaign in which Orchard Town participates with a number of other towns. Many of the organizations, of course, are not limited to North Village or Orchard Town members. The Fire Department is theoretically an all-town affair, but it has separate branches in each of the population centers. The firehouse used to be open and used to be a popular meeting place for men to play cards, including men not members of the Fire Department. Now it is much less used than formerly. In other parts of Orchard Town the Couple's Club, which periodically gives parties at the homes of its members, is connected with a church; however, in North Village this is not so. One informant said that this was because of some Catholic members who would not be able to attend if the club should become connected with a church. The Community Center is organized for the entire town, but it is located in North Village, and more North Village people participate in it than those from other parts of town. This has been very recently organized, and it is too early to describe its permanent functions and its membership. The Women's Club was limited ostensibly to North Village and a small nearby township during the period of our study. There is another Women's Club for the rest of Orchard Town. The Women's Club had about 70 members, 7 officers or directors, and 24 committees of one or more members each. There were also a few honorary and complimentary members.

None of the associations in Orchard Town are formally socially exclusive, although certain of them contain a somewhat larger proportion of high-status members than others. This reflects the official denial of social-class distinctions characteristic of small New England towns. Church membership, which often reflects such distinction, does so to a certain extent in Orchard Town as a whole but less so in North Village. Nearly all the Protestant families living in this section go to the local Baptist church rather than to the more prestigeful Unitarian and Episcopal churches in other parts of the town. Several high-status families go to the latter, however.

Although the formal social structure of North Village is open and democratic and there are no organized and self-conscious social classes, there is nevertheless considerable range in occupation and education, two of the more direct indices of socio-economic status. It has been previously noted that occupations range, from semiskilled to professional. Education shows a similar variation. The fathers of our sample varied in their educational background from grammar school only to college graduates. Table 1 shows the educational backgrounds of the parents of our sample.

As might be expected, most husbands and wives had similar educational backgrounds. Nine of the 24 had reached an identical level. Interestingly enough, women who had more schooling than their husbands outnumbered by 9 to 5 men who had more schooling than their wives.

Table 1. The educational background of the mothers and fathers of our sample

	MOTHERS	FATHERS
College plus graduate school	2	0
College graduate	2	5
Some college	6	5
High school plus business or vocational training	4	3
High school graduate	9	10
Some high school	1	0
Grade school or less	0	1

Using an adaptation of the formula developed by Warner, Meeker et al. (1949) to estimate socio-economic status from education and occupation, the range of the families of our sample was from upper lower to upper middle class, with the bulk falling into upper lower or lower middle—what some sociologists combine under the term "the common man."

The occupations listed by the members of the senior high school class in 1954 in the yearbook as their ambitions give a rough picture of the rank to which high school students aspire. Occupations of high rank include: hotel manager (1), accountant (1), engineer (4), interior decorator (1). Occupations of moderate rank would include military (4), mechanic or machinist (2), farmer (1) conservation officer (1). One boy also listed his ambition to become a motion picture projectionist, which seems somewhat lower than the others. Ambitions of the girls all were rather moderate: 8 office workers, 6 teachers, 2 nurses, 2 airline hostesses, 1 lab technician. One wanted to do something with horses; another had listed no ambition, which perhaps meant to get married.

Courses taken by the senior class in 1954 also give some indication of aspired rank. Eight boys were taking straight college courses, 4 were taking a college commercial course, and 4 were taking a general course, a total of sixteen boys. Of 23 girls, 8 were taking a straight college course, 12 a college commercial course, 3 a general course. The boys are about equally divided between a college course and other courses. The girls are about twice as many "other" as straight college course.

The belief that men and women are ideally equal is widespread. This does not mean that they are equally suited or expected to do the same things, but it does mean that there is very little apparent difference in privileges between the sexes. This is partially true because women's status depends in large part on the men with whom they are associated or to whom they are related. It may also be true that a woman without a man in her nuclear family suffers in prestige. We can say that the things women do, the roles they play, do not in themselves affect their status unless they do them especially poorly. Their status, instead, depends on whose child or whose wife they happen to be. It is very difficult to detect any considerable difference in status between a man and his wife in a given household. There is some feeling that since the status of the entire family depends in large measure on the status of the man, he should be helped, kept happy, or whatever may be necessary to enable him to boost the status of the family. On the other hand, most families would not endure quietly any great presumptiveness on the part of the man of the family.

In spite of relative equality of status, the roles of men and women in the community are largely separated. The important town officers as well as the important officials of state government are nearly always men. Women, however, hold certain offices which are considered appropriate for women. For instance, there are women holding positions of library trustee and there have been women candidates elected for the school board and the welfare board. However, there apparently has never been a woman selectman, a woman moderator, or a woman town clerk. In the church, also, the most important church officers— the trustees, the deacons, and the minister—have always been men. There are other positions, however, in the church organization which women may hold, such as superintendent of the Sunday School.

Economically women's primary responsibility is supposed to be the home. Many women work, bringing in extra cash, in addition to their work as housewife, but the men are supposed to be the main bread-winner. The total family status is considered to be higher if the woman does not work for cash.

There is a tendency in the home for major expenditures to be decided on jointly by husband and wife. However, this varies considerably from family to family. Women exercise the main control over the regular expenses of running the household.

Women have more to do with education than men do, up through the sixth grade at least. Schoolteachers in the lower grades are all women, as are the principals. The mothers of the schoolchildren also appear to take more interest than the fathers. There are room mothers who represent the parents at school but no room fathers. Women are also active in the Parent Teachers Association, although there is a tradition in Orchard Town of having a male for president of the PTA.

Polite manners require a man to show respect for a woman. He is supposed to stand when a woman enters the room, open doors for her, and let her precede him into a room. Training in the practice of "girls first" starts at an early age in the home and is carried on in the school.

The sex-role distinctions extend down into childhood from about the sixth year. Boys are supposed to act aggressive, cause more trouble, be rougher and more athletic than girls. Girls are expected to stay out of fights but to be verbally quite aggressive. Boys are expected to be more interested in things than in personalities and, therefore, less sensitive than girls. Girls and women are expected to grow and mature more quickly than men. One informant stated, "Girls are grown up at 16, but men not until 40." Girls are eager to attend the ballroom dancing class, while the "less mature" boys are reluctant. Although boys are troublesome creatures as youths, in maturity it is often jokingly remarked that the reverse is true, for instance, in one joke two men were talking about their wives. The first said, "Mine is an angel." The second man said, "Boy, you're lucky! Mine is still living." The fighting of boyhood is not expected to continue into manhood, while the cattiness of girlhood is said to increase with age.

One may also note that girls sometimes wear boys' clothes, either clothes actually belonging to a male member of their family or clothes made for women but in imitation of men's clothes, such as slacks. The reverse does not occur. Also, at one of the high school dances some couples were composed of two girls, but no couple was observed consisting of two boys. One of the faculty expressed disapproval of pairs of girls dancing but said that it was difficult to ban this completely as long as the girls were allowed to buy single tickets to the dances, which some do.

In sum, men and women are difficult to compare regarding status. Their roles are different, but the scales of prestige for them are so ambiguous that either sex can and does, usually in fun, claim priority.

☆
☆
☆

Chapter 5

Property

Few people in Orchard Town consider themselves rich or wealthy, but nearly all of them are fairly well off. One indication of the view which people of North Village hold of their economic status is that one of the Sunday School teachers took her class on a special trip to a city mission or social work agency to see "poor" children.

Main streets inside the village, schools, firehouses, libraries, greens, the dump, police cars, fire engines and the town hall are owned by the town. Management of these properties and their construction are fought over bitterly in the town meetings. Any mismanagement is highly criticized. Taxpayers dislike spending their dollars on mistakes. New taxes have to be levied and bonds issued to pay for new town properties. As far as the schools are concerned, the state pays a large share of the cost of their construction and operation. In return, the state has something to say about their management. Townspeople do not like this aspect of state aid.

Many of the stores are owned by local people who also manage them. There is also a business block in town which is owned by a landlord who rents these properties to store managers. The factories in Orchard Town are not owned by residents of the town. Businessmen from other communities have purchased factory buildings in Orchard Town because of reasonable rents and available labor. Storage and warehouses are owned by Orchard Town families.

The major property of most families consists of the house which they occupy with its furnishings and the land on which it is built with perhaps some extra land, a car, some business equipment if they are in business for themselves, usually some savings, and insurance policies. Of the 24 families in our sample, all but two owned or were buying their living quarters. A few families in town, including two in our sample, occupy part of their house and rent rooms or apartments to other individuals for additional income. Property is valued not only in itself but also as a sign of relative social status. The most important kinds of property for this purpose are house, house furnishings, car, and clothes.

Many landowners have a jealous regard for their property rights. This does not always mean, however, that any person walking on another's land is regarded as trespassing, for the town is "open" for hunting. That is, an owner must post his land with "no hunting" signs to prevent others from legally hunting upon it. Some owners of tracts of undeveloped land have posted their property against hunting, but these are in a minority.

There is now a zoning law restricting certain types of construction, but a sizable minority were opposed to the passing of this law on the ground that it interfered with property rights. While we were in town, some surveyors from the state highway department came and surveyed for the widening of one of the streets. One landowner was disturbed when the surveyors walked on his lawn and told them they had no right to set up their equipment there without his permission. However, he relented when the surveyors told him that he could put them off but not for long since they could get a warrant if necessary. Another man pulled up a speed limit sign which the state highway department had erected by the side of the road on his lawn. He said his property extended to the road and that the road was not state property but town property anyway. Later the sign was observed in place.

Although people are free to go on undeveloped land, adults would be careful not to go into other people's yards without some good reason. Children under the age of about 14 are much freer to go into other people's yards to play or to go through them on the way to some other place. Adults would not take a short-cut across some other person's yard unless they were very close neighbors and on good terms.

Sentiment about ownership of family land or houses is found among long-time residents or natives of the town, but such people are in the minority. Nevertheless, some of these people hold a considerable part of the area of the town, and they may feel disturbed about minor changes in the landscape. One landowner, for instance, looking out the window of her ancestral home, complained to one of us that a barn about a mile away had been moved. This, she said, spoiled the view. Stories are told admiringly of a family in a nearby town owning land which the original ancestors received from the Indians and, in another town nearby, of a family who received their land from grants from one of the English kings. These are very exceptional cases, however.

At present, inheritance of property is divided among the nuclear family if possible. If there are no children, a surviving spouse inherits all property unless otherwise specified by will. If there are children, the property is usually divided giving one-third to the widow and two-thirds to the children unless otherwise specified. Real estate inherited from parents would normally be sold and converted into cash unless one of the children is living in the parental home. In this case there would probably be an attempt to give each child an equal inheritance by giving all the money or other property to the other children and by selling some of the land if there were some extra land.

The most common pattern is to convert as much of the property as possible to cash by selling it. Practically all forms of property can be sold fairly readily. At present, real estate has a relatively high value and is easily converted into cash. This is possible because of the suburban expansion into Orchard Town. One house on which we have information, for instance, was sold to the current owners by the previous owners in 1953 for a price about 80% more than the previous owners paid for it in 1946.

Since the variety of material objects is much greater in American culture than in most cultures, perhaps a word should be injected here as to the relationship of Orchard Town people to material objects. Accumulation of objects goes on in most families at a very fast rate. Those living in old houses, which often have storage sheds, have a greater opportunity to keep objects which are no longer functional in a particular household. Occasionally, if some outsider has need of some of these objects, they are given away. Most of the time they are neglected or forgotten. Most are no longer in style. However, being old and out-dated are not always disadvantages and, in this area, often raise the value of an object. Community organizations have fairs and auctions to which such objects may be donated. This keeps a certain number of the objects in circulation. Other such objects sometimes are thrown in the town dump, where they may be rescued by those who want them. In this, rescuers are often especially proud of getting something for nothing, and the object starts over again its round from living room to attic to dump.

Expensive equipment is not acquired lightly or hastily. Long-range plans are generally made for the gradual accumulation of money enough to buy a new car or washing machine or a camera. There is some feeling that with the acquisition of the next object, life will be much more pleasant. Some of these expensive items are purely functional, but more often a more expensive item is particularly aesthetically pleasing or is important in achieving or maintaining status by expressing "good" taste.

Occasionally eccentric individuals are found who seem to have been overtrained in the accumulation of property and would be regarded as misers by the townspeople. One old woman, for instance, is said to have filled her room up with a large amount of old newspapers which she saved. Even her bed was partly covered with piles of these newspapers.

Wealthy people are possibly more often the object of gossip than are people who are not wealthy. Perhaps a very small amount of awe and respect is given them by adults. Children may be warned to avoid trespassing on their property more than that of others.

☆
☆
☆

Chapter 6

Political Organization

Orchard Town, like other towns in the United States, has a complex political structure. All political statuses, town, state, and national, are, in theory at least, either elective or appointive. There are no ascriptive statuses. Persons appointed to political positions are supposed to be appointed on the basis of their qualifications, although it is recognized that personal relationships also play an important part. Persons elected to office are also supposed to be chosen by the voters for their qualifications, although here again it is recognized that the personal appeal of the candidate and his relationship with members of his constituency play an important part in his election.

The informal power structure of the Orchard Town local government corresponds fairly well with the formal power structure. Other things being equal, the voice of the financially successful probably carries more weight in the town meetings than that of the financially unsuccessful person. There is some feeling that wealth and success are a fairly good measure of intelligence. Counterbalancing this, however, is the feeling that wealth may be a sign of stinginess or concentrated pursuit of one's own self-interest.

Until quite recently there was a feeling that town officials should be people of long-time residence. The older residents still retain this feeling, but because of the large influx of new residents, this sentiment is no longer as significant politically as it was perhaps ten years ago. The old residents have an advantage with respect to their real estate taxes. Real estate values have not been reassessed for taxes for a number of years, although real estate values have risen considerably over this period. There is no formal organization of either the new people or the old, which lessens the effect of either as a block.

More significant than a split between new and old are the splits which occur, or have occurred, on a number of important issues brought up at the town meetings in the history of the town. Some of those listed by the local historian include: the location of the railroad, bounty for Civil War soldiers, site of the high school, zoning, and the formation of a regional school district.

Although all political status is theoretically achievable, the townspeople have elected members of one family to be town clerk for several generations. We might speak of this as an informal ascribed office. Note that the service aspect of the town clerk job is more prominent than the power aspect, which may explain why the people have not demanded a change in this office. There is no doubt, moreover, that members of this family would not continue to be elected if they showed any major abuse of their office or if they were obviously incompetent. This situation calls attention to the fact that for many of the town offices, theoretically elective, there is usually only one candidate nominated.

Important town issues are decided at the town meetings. At these an elected town moderator presides. Other elected officials sit at the front of the meeting house and are frequently requested to or voluntarily give pertinent information on the issues which are to be considered. All voters in the town are eligible to attend the meeting and to speak freely on any issue which is of interest to them. Each year there is an annual town meeting and usually several special town meetings. Minor decisions and the implementation of decisions made at the town meeting are handled by the Board of Selectmen or the appropriate town official or committee. The town moderator presides but has no other duties, as such, and is not a member of the Board of Selectmen.

There is a total of about 50 elected town officers, counting a number of trustees of the town funds. And, in addition to these, there are about 90 appointed officers, the appointments being made by the selectmen.

A list of the functions of the town would include the following: the gathering of taxes and license fees, especially real estate taxes; the assessing of real estate for tax purposes; the running of the schools from first grade through high school; the maintaining of surfaced and lighted town roads and taking care of the trees along these roads; the maintaining of the fire department with several branches; the maintaining of a police force to preserve law and order and protect property. There is a board of health which is responsible for the sanitation of the town, which includes garbage collection and supervision of the town dump and also control of contagious diseases. There are also a town library, a town forest, and two town cemeteries. The town maintains various records, including records of birth, marriages, and deaths. The town supervises national, state, and town elections for its citizens. Of the various functions of the town government in 1954, roughly the following outlays of town funds were made: education took nearly half, police and fire departments and related function took 12%, charities 10% (this being especially for old age assistance), road maintenance 7%, Board of Health activities 4%, general government 3%, and the remainder miscellaneous.

Most town meetings and meetings of the various committees of the town officials operate with rather formal procedures, and full records are kept. Participants often bring up points of order. At one town meeting which we attended, one citizen maintained that the whole meeting was illegal, because it had not been properly called, in view of some obscure requirement which no one else seemed to know about.

The town is one small unit in a much larger political structure which extends to the federal or national level. The town is divided into three precincts as previously mentioned. There is a water district which includes North Village and parts of the rest of the town, but not the entire town. It also includes parts of a neighboring town. The political structure of the water district is modeled on the town government. During our residence, the town voted to form a regional school district with a neighboring town. This enabled greater financial assistance from the state for the operation of schools, especially the high school.

The town is one of a number of towns in a county, but the county is politically unimportant. Certain courts are organized on a county basis, and the agricultural extension service is organized for the county.

The state government is considerably more important than that of the county. The state maintains an extensive system of roads, including most of the principal roads in Orchard Town, except for short stretches in the center of villages. The state also collects taxes and licenses people in a number of occupations. It provides some financial support to the town, especially in running the schools and in charities. The town was given its original charter by the state, and changes in the charter or the by-laws have to be approved by the state attorney-general before going into effect. State laws are important in Orchard Town as well as in other towns of the state. But on the other hand, one hears expressions that the state is corrupt or that its officers are all politicians, people who lack talent except for knowing how to advance in the state or national government.

The national government is at the next level above the state government although there is also a feeling of a sort of regional unit consisting of the six New England States. This regional unit, however, has little formal organization. The national government is very important in the life of the people in Orchard Town. There is a post office, a branch of the federal government, in each of the three village centers. The federal government levies a large income tax.

The military activity of the national government is of concern to most males in Orchard Town. Most able-bodied men of the proper age have served in the Armed Services during World War II and younger men have prospects of Selective Service.

The people in Orchard Town have a part in electing representatives to the state and national legislatures. They are interested in both state and national affairs. A number of people are concerned about getting people out to vote in order to throw the total state vote to the Republican Party. There are no similar Democratic workers in the town. Party affiliations are not formally involved in the town elections, although there is some feeling that there is something strange about a man who is not a Republican.

There are many more Republicans than Democrats in the town, and apparently some who vote Democratic do not reveal this for political or business reasons. Also, some people moving into town from the city who were originally Democrats are reported to have shifted to the Republican Party after several years of residence in town. One old-time resident of the town said, "There are about 50 Democrats in Orchard Town I think." This would be out of a total population, children included, of nearly 5000. Actually, the number of people who voted in 1952 for Eisenhower in the whole town amounted to over 1700 and the number who voted for Stevenson was about 350. The proportion in North Village was roughly comparable to this. It can be seen that this informant's estimate of the number of Democrats was too low, but it indicates the political atmosphere of the town.

Most of the voters in Orchard Town regard themselves as at least moderately conservative politically. Although they are suspicious at times of big business, they are even more so of communism or socialism. They are concerned about the interference of the national government in state affairs and the interference of the state in town affairs. While they recognize the need for both state and national governments, they do not want state or national governments to expand in influence. The townspeople feel that they, individually and jointly, should be allowed to take care of their own affairs as much as possible.

One of the ministers in town reported that during the period of great concern with the national security and communist infiltration, he had commented unfavorably on Senator McCarthy in a sermon. He cited the sermon as one of the few that he had given on which he had personally received unfavorable comment from members of his congregation. As far as we could determine, there are no Communists in Orchard Town. Yet, before our arrival in town, it is reported that one of the local political leaders had accused a number of people of being Communists or at least Communist sympathizers. How extreme the actual informal accusations were we cannot say, since those not in sympathy with the accusations would tend to exaggerate them to make them appear to be more absurd.

There are few formal rules of respect for holders of political office except at town meetings and under certain circumstances. At town meetings, the officials and other persons who expect to make speeches or motions usually are dressed in dark suits, speak of each other as mister, and use somewhat parliamentary language. When speaking from the floor, one man may refer to another by his official title, "the Chairman of the School Committee," rather than by his name, but this is by no means a hard and fast rule. Outside of official proceedings there is not much more respect shown for holders of political office other than that to which they would be entitled as adult citizens in good standing.

❦
❦
❦

Chapter 7

Social Control

Informal social control in Orchard Town is generally indirect, in the form of gossip, avoidance, or exclusion, rather than direct. We observed no instances in which one adult publicly criticized another to his face except in a bantering or teasing manner. Spouses sometimes criticized one another in the presence of guests, but this was felt to be improper behavior and was embarrassing to the guests. Gossip, although not intended as such, is in fact very effective in ensuring value consensus and conformity. Mrs. A tells Mrs. B what she thinks of Mrs. C for leaving her children without a baby sitter. Whether or not Mrs. B agrees, she seldom will challenge Mrs. A on her statement, but the exchange will influence Mrs. B if at a later date she is tempted to leave her children without a sitter. She will know what Mrs. A will say about her.

Informal ostracism is also frequently used as a means of social control in Orchard Town. This takes the form of "cutting," "being cool to," or failing to invite to a social gathering one whose behavior is disapproved.

A final indirect method of social control which is sometimes employed in Orchard Town consists of the criticism of someone to one of his friends or relatives with the expectation that this will in some way be passed on to the deviant.

Children may occasionally function as agents of adult social control, since they sometimes repeat remarks of their parents which the parents would make only among themselves. They, also, do not have the hesitation of adults to use direct criticism. It was reported, also, that the children used to tease one man cruelly for his drinking. It was believed by some that this contributed to his final suicide.

What sort of matters are the concern of gossip, criticism, or informal social control? One of the most important is lack of industriousness. An able-bodied man who does not work and is not striving to better himself and the position of his family would be shunned and regarded with scorn unless he had enough income to maintain his family and himself comfortably. Even then, he would come in for some criticism if he did not work.

Personal cleanliness and a general cleanliness of the home are another subject of informal social control. A person who did not mow his lawn, for instance, would be severely criticized. People also ought to keep their hedges trimmed and have dead limbs on trees removed, have their houses painted, and so forth. A woman should keep her house clean and pick up things on occasions when visitors are expected.

Excessive drinking is generally disapproved, and a large number of the older people and the regular churchgoers are opposed to any form of alcoholic beverage. Many people who do drink do so privately, deferring to the feeling of those opposed to drinking.

Considerable informal pressure is exerted against parents of children who are disrespectful to adults, destructive of property, or in other ways deviate from the values of the community.

Prevention of crime is urged and carried out by most people in locking up property which might be stolen. One teen-age boy was urged by his mother not to tell anyone over the telephone that he was alone in the house when he was left to sit with younger siblings. Crowds of loafers are not allowed to gather. Crowds of teen-age boys are broken up if they become noisy and disorderly. At night children and women of all ages avoid going out alone, unless they are driving in a car.

Most of the formal law enforcement in Orchard Town is concerned with traffic offenses. In 1954 the police reported nearly 500 arrests and prosecutions for various motor vehicle offenses and less than 30 offenses of all other types. Common punishment for motor vehicle offenses is a fine. For driving under the influence of liquor, the punishment is the loss of license either temporarily or permanently. For serious motor vehicle offenses, the punishment, of course, may be imprisonment. This is rather rare. Not all of the 500 traffic offenses involved residents of Orchard Town. Many of them were no doubt people of other towns who were driving through. However, it must be remembered that people of Orchard Town themselves do a lot of driving through other towns where they are subject to arrest for traffic offenses, so the figure is not quite so misleading as it may seem.

In 1954, of the less than 30 miscellaneous offenses, 11 were for drunkenness, and no other category was larger than 2. Orchard Town people feel that crimes are, as a rule, committed by outsiders or by young boys who are potential delinquents. There is a widespread sentiment that young boys and men, especially in the big cities, but some in the town as well, are getting out of control; "You never heard of the crimes then that you do nowadays."

Three institutions are particularly used for formal social control. They are the police, the court, and the jail. A generation ago in Orchard Town there was no regular police force. Certain men were elected Constables. The job of Constable was and still is a supplementary one, and today these men do very little. They are active only on special occasions. There are also two full-time and two part-time policemen who are employed on a regular basis.

Until recently all police were elected, and their continuity in office depended on public approval—approval of both their integrity as a policeman and their reasonableness as a human being. A policeman's job does not pay unusually well. Compared with other jobs in private industry or business, it is a respectable job but not one of high prestige. Orchard Town people feel confident of the integrity of their own policemen, but it is generally recognized that police in the larger cities can often be bribed into not giving tickets for traffic violations.

The nearest court is in an adjoining town. The most common contact with the court system for the people of Orchard Town is for traffic offenses and after that for civil suits. Few residents of Orchard Town are involved in criminal cases either as defendants or witnesses. Many of them serve on juries from time to time, however. Potential civil suits involving financial damages are often settled informally out of court. People express the opinion that lawyers are expensive and that the damages awarded in court are liable to be excessive.

There is no jail in Orchard Town, although there is a state penal institution in a nearby town. Orchard Town people have practically no contact with this institution. Television and movies, of course, present images of both courts and jails which are realistic and taken as such by the children and adults. Nevertheless, there is a feeling that courts and jails are things which belong primarily to the city and not to small towns. The police rarely have occasion to take drastic action against local people—adults or children. Cases of North Village children being sent to the reform school are not frequent and have involved families who are more or less marginal socially.

Both young people and adults feel that teenagers of the town, especially the young men and boys, are tempted to become "delinquent" because "there is nothing to do." Some examples of delinquency cited were: putting a lighted cigarette in a mail box and painting the windshield of a car. One informant said that one boy was sent to reform school after an outburst of such activity and that things then quieted down.

※
※
※

Chapter 8

Religion

In North Village there are two churches, one Protestant, which is officially a Baptist church but in practice is largely a community church, and one Roman Catholic church. People of various denominational backgrounds attend the Baptist church. Most people regard blurring of denominational boundaries among Protestants as a good thing. At the communion service, for instance, in the North Village Protestant church, the minister regularly invites visitors, regardless of denomination, to join in the consumption of the grape juice and bread. The North Village church participates in a regional group of Protestant churches as well as in a regional group of Baptist churches. It is our impression that the activity connected with the denominational group is remaining about constant, while the activity with other nearby Protestant churches in the local group is increasing. For example, the local Protestant churches exchange ministers. If one of their ministers becomes sick, they may get a minister from a nearby church of another denomination. They also hold joint services at Christmas, Thanksgiving, and so on.

Most of the population of Orchard Town, perhaps 90%, is nominally Protestant. Lines of cleavage between the various Protestant denominations are not too sharp. It is not unusual for a family or an individual to shift from one denomination to another because of personal relationships with the minister or other people in a church. The various Protestant churches in the three centers of Orchard Town also hold joint services and cooperate in other ways.

There is little cooperation between Catholic and Protestants as religious groups. At town affairs, the high school graduation, Catholic and Protestant ministers may be together to offer prayers, one offering the invocation and the other the final blessing. In daily life, however, there are many social and business contacts between individual Catholics, especially the older residents, and Protestants.

Although we were told that with respect to our study, "The Catholics don't like to be left out of things," we chose not to study the Catholic families because of the difference of religious influence this would introduce. Accordingly, the Catholic church in North Village will not be discussed here.

At the North Village church the average attendance at the Sunday morning service has varied from 60 to 100 for the last decade. Considering the large Protestant population in the town, this is not many. There are more children in Sunday School, over 200 being enrolled there. Many residents and members are too old to attend church often. Others attend church very irregularly. The variation in attendance at Sunday Service during the last decade is the result of turnover in ministers. At first, many people attend to hear what the new man has to say. Then later they lose interest or sometimes get into feuds with the minister. Some people may stop attending church or they may transfer to another Protestant church in a nearby community. There is competition between the different churches for audiences and members. Many people start attending church when their children are old enough to start going to Sunday School. One woman said that she had transferred to another church because of the emphasis on Hell and damnation in the Baptist Sunday School. Actually, there is little mention of hell or damnation in the Baptist church in either the Sunday morning service or the Sunday School, but such are the rationalizations that lead to shifting membership.

At present, about the only obvious doctrinal difference of the local Baptist church with other churches is that it encourages baptism by immersion. However, members now may join without baptism on a simple confession of faith. This change was foreshadowed by earlier action. For instance, in 1920, members of other denominations were allowed to become affiliated members of the North Village church on presentation of a letter confirming that they had been previous members of another church of another denomination. In the 1940's persons of other denominations were allowed to become full members on presentation of a letter. The final step, taken during our study, was to allow persons who had never been a member of any church before to become full members of the North Village church on simple profession of faith. Children who desired to become members of the church, having gone through the Sunday School, would, however, be inducted with baptism.

The official church membership in the last decade has varied from 100 to 160. There has been less variation in the church membership than in attendance. In general, there have been considerably more members than there has been average attendance in the church. Not all the official members attend regularly, but some nonmembers attend on a fairly regular basis. In fact, perhaps half of those attending each Sunday are nonmembers.

The church is largely managed by the board of trustees, who look after the church property, and the board of deacons, who supervise the religious activities. The minister is important as a leader but is formally subject to the congregation and its officers. There are many special committees and offices. Most members of the church have been a member of one or more of these committees. These officers are all elected, but normally there is only one ticket. The Sunday School now is under the Religious Education Committee.

North Village Protestants give most of their attention to two supernatural beings, God and Jesus. While there is an occasional mention of the Trinity, the third member, the Holy Ghost, is rarely mentioned specifically. Both God and Jesus are seen as having infinite mercy. They are forgiving, but on the other hand they give little, if any, practical help. The principle difference between them is that one is the Father and the other the Son, and that Jesus the Son was at one time human. The Devil and Hell are seldom mentioned, although one minister said that he felt the idea of Hell was needed. If the question were raised, there might be some argument as to whether the Devil existed or not, but at any rate, it was agreed that he is not important and that children should hear little of him. On one occasion when the Devil happened to be mentioned in a Sunday School lesson, some of the children expressed surprise on the grounds that there really was no Devil. Angels are occasionally mentioned to children in Sunday School but little elsewhere. Saints are hardly mentioned, and there appears to be no way of adding to the number of saints.

If asked specifically, most people would probably admit that God does not help people to succeed or make them rich and probably does not cure sickness, although there is less consistency about this last. As a minister once put it, "The symbol of Christianity is a cross and not a rabbit's foot; it is no guarantee of any worldly success or even happiness."

The divinity of Jesus seems to be acknowledged or at least not contradicted openly by most churchgoers. However, considerable attention is given to the human nature of Jesus. One Sunday School teacher, talking about Jesus as a child said, "I don't mean to say that He was perfect. He was a normal person and I am sure He got into little tiffs, but still He was somewhat different from us for He was a supernatural being . . . so let's try to be like Him."

Most people do not seem to regard the Bible as infallible, although statements are made about the New Testament being the Church's guide. A sermon by the minister in which he said that he, personally, did not regard the New Testament as infallible, not to mention the whole Bible, did not seem to arouse any undue comment from the congregation. A high value is placed on the independence of both the congregation and individuals to decide what they want to believe and practice. A belief in immortality is general in the sense that if they were questioned, most people would probably subscribe to it, but it does not appear to be very important in that it is not often mentioned in the sermons or in the Sunday School material. This seems to be a belief which is activated mainly at funerals, but it does not seem to motivate individual daily behavior, since there is little belief that one will be punished for his sins after death or permanently confined to Hell or to some form of suffering for his sins.

In religious and Sunday School literature and in the sermons, little distinction is made between male and female ideals. However, the religious teachings are more consistent with female than male ideals as they are found in the culture at large. An emphasis on not retaliating or not resisting evil is found in the religious teaching which conflicts with the male ideal of self-respect. Self-respect is maintained by not letting anyone push you around, by retaliating with injury. When we asked for opinions on this conflict at a church parents' meeting, one father said, "We must read between the lines of the Bible." Usually more women than men attend church, and, also, more women are Sunday School teachers. Men who are Sunday School teachers are usually the husbands of women who are also Sunday School teachers.

In the past, New England Protestant churches have been opposed to drinking and smoking, although in the far distant past ministers were expected to receive part of their salary in rum. The temperance movement, which was strong during the late nineteenth and early twentieth century, is now mild. Many members of the church do not drink, and there are no ashtrays in the church building, but there is no active, organized temperance movement within the church. Moreover, some members of the church do drink in private or in appropriate company. Many smoke.

Legally there are so-called "blue laws" restricting work and disturbances on Sundays. Only a few adults take these very seriously. One town official told of a complaint which one citizen had made about another man: "He was hammering so that I could not even light my pipe or read my paper; don't we have any blue laws in this town?" The official commented that this man had just wanted to complain, so he let him and that was enough. However, the official himself felt that if anyone had noisy work of this sort to do, he would be advised to do it in his backyard on Sundays. Many of the parents observed had had restrictions on their own behavior on Sundays which they would not now attempt to enforce on themselves or their children. This is a noticeable change within the last couple of generations. One woman said that although her parents were not churchgoers, she still felt guilty about playing cards on Sunday. "You are supposed to grow Devil's horns and hooves for playing cards on Sundays, my mother always said."

The church also emphasizes the value of service and charity. Missionary activity is felt by many to be important and valuable, although the interest in missionary activity is expressed primarily through contributions of cash and does not as a rule involve actual proselytizing.

During the life of an individual, five points may be marked by religious services. The first occasion occurs shortly after birth when an infant's parents bring him to church for a service of parental dedication. The next point, perhaps roughly at puberty, is baptism. After this comes marriage, and after giving birth to children, the individual participates again in parental dedication as a parent. Finally, when he dies, he is given a funeral. It is not necessary for a person to participate in any of these services to be regarded as nominally Protestant.

In the early days of the North Village church, baptism was a more impressive ceremony than it is now. It was then carried out in a brook near the town. Now it is carried out in a tank or "baptistry" with water of controlled temperature. The tank is located at the front of the church, but in such a position that the audience cannot see the actual immersion. Except when in use, the tank is covered over by the floor. Most of the children in the Sunday School seem to be amused by the idea of baptism. This is an attitude which they probably obtained from their parents, who in many cases are not Baptists, and also from their playmates. When a child is baptized, he becomes a member of the church. He is not supposed to be baptized before he reaches an age when he may make a decision. This is usually after the age of 12. Theoretically children may attend communion before this, but they are discouraged if they do not "understand."

No church marriage took place while we were making our study, and none had occurred for sometime before that. It is possible that the minister had married some individuals privately that we did not hear about. Church marriages are felt to be exciting occasions, however, when they do occur.

Church funerals also are fairly rare. It seems more common to hold funerals at an undertaker's establishment or at the deceased's home. However, a few church funerals did occur while we were in North Village.

The principal religious activity of the North Village church is the regular Sunday morning service. One Sunday a month, communion is held. When we came to North Village, a Wednesday-evening prayer meeting was also held, but few people attended it, and finally it was abolished. Sunday morning services resemble other Protestant church services in the area, but the Wednesday-evening prayer meeting was a little more specialized in that it consisted largely of prayers given by the members of the congregation present. People of other denominational background did not seem to participate in this meeting much.

There are two ladies' auxiliary groups, one primarily for the older women which meets during the day for sewing and the other for young women with children which generally meets in the evening. Both groups sponsor luncheons or suppers, and programs with invited speakers who talk on subjects of general interest, especially travel, gardens, and "the home." A men's auxiliary group in the church carries on similar activities, although not as frequently. It is the official sponsor of one of the Boy Scout troops in the town. The men try to meet one evening a month except during the summer. Neither of the men's or women's groups do very much directly in the way of religious activity. They sometimes make some kind of contribution to the church facilities. For instance, on one occasion it is recorded that the ladies' group provided carpets and cushions for the pews. Religious elements in their meetings are usually restricted to an initial prayer, a final benediction, and grace before meals.

While we were living in North Village for our study, one of the Congregational churches in another part of Orchard Town and a Universalist church each put on church shows in the North Village

Women's Club building. The purpose of these was to raise funds for improvements to the church buildings. It was said that the Baptist church did not put on a church show itself because of the feeling of some of the older people that this was an inappropriate way for a church to raise money. But some members of the Baptist church participated in the other church shows, and many also attended both shows, so the sentiment against church shows cannot be said to be very strong or general. The Catholic church and some of the other Protestant churches in and around Orchard Town also have whist parties as a fund-raising activity. The Baptist church does not have these.

The Baptist church raises money by an annual bazaar or fair put on by the ladies' auxiliary at which home-prepared food, handiwork, and other small articles are sold. Direct appeals for money are also favored. While we were in the village, the North Village church put on a building-fund campaign. This was organized by a national organization which specializes in showing churches how to get money from their members most effectively. The essence of the plan was to obtain pledges from people or regularly weekly contributions for a period of roughly three years. Also certain individuals, including the canvassers, were supposed to announce their pledges publicly. Some people expressed some embarrassment about this, although most of the active church members seemed to feel that the plan was necessary and did not openly oppose it.

⚜
⚜
⚜

Chapter 9

Health and Medicine

The residents of Orchard Town subscribe to the scientific theories of Western medicine to explain disease. Although only the doctors are expected to control medical knowledge, every adult in Orchard Town has a rich store of convictions about the cause and cure of all but the most unusual diseases.

Germs are thought to cause most diseases. Germs are sensed as tiny invisible animals that swarm around sick people, particularly when they sneeze, cough, or exhale. For this reason, sick people are generally isolated and avoided. A person who sneezes is expected to cover his mouth and nose and to turn the head while coughing. Germs are also believed to infest dirt of any kind and feces in particular. For this reason, children at an early age are taught to wash their hands before eating.

Despite all these precautions, a person may get sick because his resistance is weak, and the attacking germs can overcome his defenses. This condition is generally described as being "run down" and may be caused by a faulty diet, worry, or by "overdoing things," for example, working or playing too hard. In addition, susceptibility to certain specific diseases may be influenced by prior action of the patient. Thus colds and pneumonia are thought to be brought on by getting one's feet wet or sitting in drafts or not dressing warmly enough. Some people believe that eating too many sweets or too much sugar will bring on diabetes, swallowing gum will cause appendicitis, and improper diet during adolescence leads to acne.

Good health is thought to be engendered by a good diet, proper exercise, and the avoidance of excess. Many people also take vitamin pills or other elixirs presumed to prevent "tired blood" or "that run-down feeling." Talks on diet are popular with women's groups. At one of these, the speaker asserted that children's I.Q. scores were greatly influenced by nutrition. "If you feed your child properly, he will do better in school and later life as well," she stated. She also quoted with approval the following motto on overeating, "Always be hungry, never relax, or you'll be sorry."

Regular bowel movements are thought to be necessary for good health. Constipation is believed by many to be dangerous, and medicines are taken to counteract it.

No matter how one feels, a person is not defined as being really sick unless he has a fever. For this reason a thermometer is standard equipment in any household. So strong is the New England value placed on work and achievement that anyone who stays home from school or work is considered to be a malingerer unless he can show a temperature of over 100 degrees. When one has a fever, however, he is defined as being sick, goes to bed, and has someone call the doctor. If the patient is defined as having a minor illness, he is treated at home, but if he is seriously ill, he will be taken to a hospital.

The common cold is epidemic in Orchard Town during the winter and is considered to be a minor ailment, one often treated by home remedies. People have different cold cures which they favor. There is a constant succession of remedies. Someone tries a new remedy and recommends it to friends, and it becomes popular but later may be abandoned for a still newer remedy. The statement is also heard at times, "Nothing can cure the common cold."

Smoking is believed to be a potential cause of bad health. Children are not allowed to smoke and not allowed to purchase cigarettes by law. Children are told that smoking will stunt their growth, although one boy in our sample, age 9, calmly denied this. Orchard Town people shared the recent national concern about smoking as a cause of lung cancer, and some people cut down on their cigarette smoking during our study.

The people of Orchard Town regard their town as a relatively healthy place compared to the cities and also compared to some other towns in the general vicinity. According to the town report for 1954, there were 44 deaths that year, the youngest person being 43, the oldest person 93, and the median being 72. Deaths of younger people have occurred in other years, but once a person is born, he has an excellent chance of surviving to adulthood.

The town and state governments officially subscribe to the importance of the early detection of physical disorders and disease. Schoolchildren are given periodical physical examinations, special eye and hearing examinations, and, recently, dental examinations. The parents are notified of the results of these examinations. Until recently there was no dentist in Orchard Town, and this meant that the teeth of many children were not well cared for. Children showed some resistance to wearing glasses when the glasses were shown to be necessary by the eye examination. Boys "don't want to be bothered," while the girls tend to be concerned about glamour, at least at high school age. The school nurse reported that the recent decorative varieties of glasses had made eyeglasses more popular with the girls and that it was also possible to motivate the boys to wear glasses by saying, "Don't you want to drive a car?"

Small pox vaccinations are required for schoolchildren by state law and generally are accepted by the parents. Nearly 90% of the parents with children in the first two grades gave their consent for their children to receive the Salk polio vaccine in 1955 in spite of the concern that it might accidently produce polio.

Dread diseases of past generations, such as tuberculosis and typhoid fever, have been largely eliminated or controlled when they occur. Certain childhood diseases are regarded as almost inevitable: chicken pox, measles, mumps, and whooping cough. Serious complications from these now seem to be better controlled than they were formerly, and there appears to be much less concern over a long quarantine period for children with these diseases than there was formerly. A considerable number of children in our sample had their tonsils removed or were expected to have their tonsils removed to control sore throat. The children seem to accept this operation fairly well. For very young children, virus pneumonia and respiratory infections are a source of worry. One reason here is that three young babies, less than one year old, were said to have died of virus pneumonia in the town in a recent year, two of them quite unexpectedly.

☙
☙
☙

Chapter 10

Recreation

A number of activities which might be considered adult recreation have already been considered in the discussion of voluntary associations, under Social Organization. These will not be discussed again here.

Some forms of adult recreation involve both the husband and the wife and may also involve the other members of the family. Some families invite friends or relatives over occasionally for dinner or for some sort of after-dinner refreshment in the evening or occasionally in the daytime on Sundays or holidays. During the warmer part of the year guests may be invited to a "cook-out." "Cook-out" is especially used to refer to meals in one's backyard, where families have a small stone fireplace or barbecue pit.

In the summer the whole family may drive to certain places in nearby towns which sell both bulk ice cream and fountain specialties. Often each member of the family will get something at the fountain, and the family will take home a couple of quarts of ice cream to put in the refrigerator.

Many adults go to movies fairly frequently either by themselves or with the whole family. There is now a drive-in theater in Orchard Town out in the country, near North Village, to which the whole

family may go on a warm evening. There are also conventional thea-
ters in nearby towns.

Occasionally adults, especially men, buy tickets to watch spectator
sports in the city, such as baseball, basketball, or football. Children.
especially older boys, may be taken along if the event is in the daytime.

Both men and women occasionally attend theatrical productions in
the city. Perhaps more common is attending the local church amateur
shows, of which there have been two or three a year recently. Some
people pride themselves on "never" going into the city.

Many residents of Orchard Town enjoy listening to music on television, radio, or records, but few play musical instruments. Those who
attend church sing the hymns in church, but there is also music provided by the choir. On some social occasions there is group singing of
traditional popular songs. Group leaders consider singing a good way
to get a crowd interested in interacting. At one public gathering the
following words were sung to the song, "It's a Long Road to Tipperary":

> It's a good time to get acquainted.
> It's a good time to know.
> Who is sitting close beside you.
> So just smile and say hello.
> Goodbye, chilly shoulder,
> Goodbye, glassy stare.
> When we all join in (shake hand of person next to you),
> And pull together,
> We are sure to get there.

Singing such songs seems to fulfill a general need to appear happy in
public and to have flashing smiles. Although people are often embarrassed and appear to hesitate, they usually "thaw out" and "get
into the swing of things."

Some families, especially those with children, have pets, usually
dogs. Adults treat their pets affectionately, but they often give utili-
tarian reasons for having them, for example, a dog is a good watch
dog or a cat keeps the place free of mice. Some adults enjoy bird-
watching and have bird-feeding stations outside their windows. This
seems to be more popular among long-time residents.

The telephone has become important in the recreational life of the
women in Orchard Town. Women often break their round of chores
by exchanging daily experiences, gossip, and recipes. The men tend
to feel that the telephone should be used for necessary communication
only, and, partly for this reason, the women usually call one another
while their husbands are at work.

It is said that the depot, the firehouse, and the barber shop were places where men foregathered to exchange gossip and to discuss the affairs of the town, the state, and the nation. The traditional gathering of rural America, the crackerbarrel group, no longer exists in Orchard Town. The old timers talk about the olden days with nostalgia and wonder "what the world is coming to." Many blame the radio, television, and even the automobile for this turn of events.

The depot and firehouse provided a place for men to play cards after hours. A generation ago, when the North Village barbershop had a pool table in the back room, it was a recreational gathering place for both men and boys. Now it is illegal to have pool tables and loitering in barber shops is discouraged. One of the functions of the state inspector is to make surprise visits from time to time to prevent such loitering.

The all male poker game for money is also pretty much a thing of the past. Card playing has been taken over by women as a club recreation or as a family pastime. Bridge and whist are the favorite games, and they are not played for money but for prizes provided by the hostess or the club.

Dancing is a form of recreation enjoyed by many of the younger adults and most of the teenagers. Square dancing seems to be about as popular with the adults as ballroom dancing. During our stay, few ballroom dances were held in North Village for adults. We attended what was supposed to be the first square dance ever held in the North Village Protestant church vestry. We heard no overt criticism of this, although some of the people dancing made remarks about how daring they were being.

Auctions may be regarded as a form of recreation. Although only economically important to the owner whose property is being auctioned off, the auction may be of minor economic importance to the spectators. Individuals attend not because of something they need and hope to find there but to see what interesting or curious articles may be offered for sale. Much time at auctions is devoted to the sale of miscellaneous household ornaments.

Generally there are more women than men at auctions because they are usually held during the day when men are at work. However, when men are able to attend, they also seem to enjoy themselves. Antique-shop dealers and antique collectors, which latter category includes a large part of the population, especially the women, eagerly attend auctions and often bid high prices for "genuine antiques." Some men who are handy with tools and have time available attend auctions to buy broken furniture which they repair and use or dispose of as they see fit.

The auctioneers are generally professionals who are engaged for the occasion. People go as much to watch the auctioneers as to buy things. The auctioneers deliberately spice up the proceedings with humor, of which the following are examples: "This came off the hill; nice section up there." An auctioneer offering some perfume for bidding thrust the bottle to the audience and said, "I want every lady to put a little bit on her coat, but don't any of the men put it on!"

Children also attend auctions if they are not at school. There seem to be more auctions held in the summer than in the winter. Children may enter the bidding for small articles. While the auctioneers are allowed to indulge in various sorts of humor, one sort of humor which is not allowed to either adults or children is fake or joke bidding. No violation of this rule was observed at any of the auctions. Vendors of soft drinks and coffee often attend auctions and do a thriving business.

Gardening and fixing up the yard and house are treated as recreation rather than work by many. Such matters as how to lay flagstones or the best fertilizer for roses are frequent topics of conversation between neighbors and friends.

Several athletic sports, such as skiing and swimming, are enjoyed by the whole family. Others, such as hunting and fishing, are primarily male sports. Hunting takes place in the area of scrub forest owned by the Sportsmen's Club in a relatively unsettled part of town. Deer and pheasant are the most sought-after game. During the hunting season parents living outside the area of concentrated settlement worry about their children getting shot. Two families in our sample of 24 complained of hunters discharging their weapons uncomfortably near their houses. Although this is illegal, the law is difficult to enforce. Because of increasing numbers of hunters and the irresponsibility of a few in ignoring the restrictions, there seems to be increasing sentiment for closing the town to them except when the individual property owner gives permission.

Children may not use firearms, and all adults must have licenses to fish and hunt. There are limits set by law on the size and quantity of fish and animals which may be taken.

The Sportsmen's Club organizes an annual Field Day with trap shooting contests and raffles. They sell soft drinks and food and have small-scale gambling similar to that found in carnival side shows.

There is no golf course in Orchard Town, but there are golf courses in adjoining towns; some men play golf in the summer. One mother said that golf took her husband away from their son as well as from his business. She said that the father had taken their son along as caddy, but he had more or less given this up, for he did not want the son to hear the kind of language some of his golfing friends used.

Bowling is another popular male sport. There is a bowling league connected with the church. Bowlers must also go to nearby towns, but this is not difficult by automobile.

Watching fires is a popular activity, especially for men. Large crowds of spectators are reported at fires. The voluntary fire department is said to have a waiting list of applicants to join. Fires, of course, are not a planned form of recreation, although it is often suspected that they are caused by firebugs or arsonists. When they do occur, however, they are considered as very exciting occasions which are somehow important to watch even if one is in no position to help. Children are also very interested in fires and fire engines. One 7-year-old boy told an elaborate fantasy of his experience of having attended a fire with his father. His parents, however, said that he had not attended any fire and that, although his father was willing to have him go with him, the boy was afraid to go.

It should be noted, also, that fires are always reported in detail over the local radio and in both the big city and local papers along with other disasters such as drownings, auto accidents, and plane crashes. Although most New Englanders would not admit that listening to and reading such accounts were a form of recreation, they do in fact subject themselves to this sort of information every day, and it is very often a major topic of gossip and conversation. Of all the disasters which occur in the news, fires seem to be of special interest to the citizens of Orchard Town and perhaps the most feared. One couple with two small children lived for a number of years in an old house which they considered a fire trap. During this time they slept apart with the children, the wife sleeping with the daughter and the husband with the son, so that in the event of fire they would be able to help their children to escape.

Much adult recreation, when it does occur, takes parents away from their children. It is felt that adult recreation occurring in the evening is too late for children. A few children, however, from the age of about 6 on were observed attending vaudeville types of entertainment given in the town, such as the church shows or PTA shows. These were decidedly in the minority, and most families would insist that children under high school age should go to bed.

Even when the parents have some kind of recreation in the home, such as inviting guests for dinner or for a visit in the evening, the children do not participate a great deal. If the children are present at dinner, they are expected to keep reasonably quiet. After the meal they are expected to play elsewhere—go outside if the weather is good or to their bedroom or play area.

Since much adult recreation takes place at night, the parents must get a baby sitter if they have young children up to the age of 9 or 10.

Older siblings, if there are any, may serve as baby sitters or at least eliminate the need for baby sitters. Baby sitters as a rule are paid, although there is some exchange of baby sitting among parents who are friendly with each other. Some parents seem to regard the problem of finding baby sitters—that is, not simply paying for them but finding one who will be willing to come in the evening—as difficult. Because of the baby sitting problem, having young children hinders the parents from engaging in recreation.

Within the home, watching television is considered one of the main forms of recreation. One girl noted that when television was introduced, the prediction was made that it would help bring families together again, since they would watch television in the home rather than go out for amusement and recreation. This girl felt that actually television reduces the time that the family is together, since different members of the family are interested in different programs. And when the children were concentrating on a program, they were effectively removed from interacting with the adults; evening meals were rushed in order to finish in time to watch certain television programs.

The long list of recreational activities presented above may seem tedious, but it is an indication of the amount of time that the people of Orchard Town are free from either making a living or performing rituals and attending ceremonies which are thought to be necessary for their well-being or that of the community. Providing activities for leisure time may be a problem, especially for the teenagers. The remark was made by several parents that Orchard Town was a fine place for young children, but it was not very good for teenagers or young adults. One teenager said, "There is nothing to do in this town; it's dead."

Part II

Child Training

✤
✤
✤
✤
✤
✤

Chapter 11

The Nature of the Child in Orchard Town

The community's conception of the nature of the child has important implications for the whole system of child training. This conception of the child's nature is based on the ideas about how the child learns and how he develops. While the basic philosophy behind the socialization process in this community is constant for all families, the philosophy itself allows for a wide variety of training techniques and of goals for individual children and families.

In Orchard Town, the newborn infant is thought of as a "potential." The central concept of the child as a potential involves beliefs about the inheritance of characteristics, beliefs about the influence of parental training on the child, beliefs about the influence of the social environment and education, and beliefs about stages and norms. The interrelation of these beliefs, and the influence of the conceptual system as a whole on the socialization process is the subject of this chapter.

DEFINITION OF THE CONCEPTUAL SYSTEM

The infant as a potential is thought to be a bundle of largely inherited latent traits of emotional expression and abilities for achieving goals, which can only be realized gradually as the child develops and which may be influenced by training and growth. Most of the goals available to the children and adults of this community are thought to call for particular skills and a particular personality type, both of which must develop naturally or be influenced to develop out of the latent traits in the infant's potential. Children may have a high or low potential for the development of certain skills or personality traits. The combination of both a high potential and the best environmental influences is thought to be essential to the greatest success in achieving the goals offered to the adult.

The community members are not completely aware of their own view of the child. Evidence for this philosophy, however, is abundant in the conversation and public speeches of the people. For example,

A woman: It is in the nature of children to dawdle.
Observer: What do you mean by "the nature of children"?
Woman: It is mostly inherited, although some comes from training.
A minister in a sermon: Of course we all have different potentialities within us. We can all do a lot better than we are doing if we will follow God's way [i.e., let God show us how to develop our potentialities].
A mother: Spanking doesn't work with some children. One of my brothers was like that and my mother could never understand that. . . .
A laborer: Some people are fit to be white collar and some are not.

The beliefs about the general nature of the latent features of the potential and the method of acquisition of these latent features throw considerable light on the socialization process. The latent traits in the potential are thought to have a number of general characteristics. They are thought of as (1) fluid, (2) partially concealed, (3) being both good and bad, and (4) being more or less subject to influence from without.

Keeping the potential as fluid as possible is important for allowing the child to reach an ideal maturity. Fluidity is retained by noninterference. It is felt that adult pressure may arrest development and set the child in a mold which is not the ideal expression of his potential. Some of the fluidity of the potential is seen to be retained until the death of the individual as shown by such statements as "You keep learning until

you die," and "I learn something new everyday." The potential, however, becomes gradually actualized or "set" as the child grows. In this
way people become "types." When this happens there is thought to be
little further hope of personality change or development. Depending
on the context, people in the community are able to classify adults into
various types. For example, they may be thought of as dominated by a
particular trait—"He is a hard worker." Even children become types as
shown by statements about various children: "(He) is an underhanded
stirrer-upper," "He won't harbor a grudge, he's very open," "He's the
sneaky type, quiet about everything and a trouble-maker."

The belief that the potential is in part concealed leads to great
emphasis on techniques for the discovery and disclosure of the child's
potential. The infant is thought of as possessing innate capacities
peculiar to himself which will be revealed in the natural course of his
development, subject to the influences around him. It is thought that
the potential can be developed better if it is known or divined in
advance. Divining for the potential is highly developed in the community. There are, of course, the formal tests for intelligence, personality and achievement, but there are also more subtle techniques, such
as informal questioning of the child or observing his behavior for clues.
Clues include such things as the child showing a special interest in
something (e.g., sports or animals), or doing something particularly
well (e.g., dancing, drawing, various school subjects). After the potential has been divined parents and teachers feel more secure in taking
a particular course of action in the training of the child.

Since both good and bad features are existent in the child's potential,
it follows that a child may momentarily exhibit either his good or his
bad qualities. The child is thought to be more likely to exhibit his bad
features if he is physically tired or has had "too much" excitement. It
is also felt that good and bad aspects may be exhibited for no apparent
reason. "I was just telling you what a little devil he is and today he is
an angel." This concept of the potential as containing both good and
bad aspects is related to the two schools of child training in the town.
One school is concerned, chiefly, with curbing the bad aspects of the
child's nature; the other is concerned with developing the good aspects.

Distinctions are made between the traits in the potential on the basis
of the amount of possible influence from the environment. In addition,
it is felt that strong influences must be exerted against traits which do
not go well together. The physical features of the child are thought to
be among his more rigid traits. Even these, however, are felt to be influenced somewhat by health habits. Sex, being a rigid trait, other
traits have to be influenced from the outside to develop in accordance
with the child's sex. People may say, "What a pity! She should have

been a boy." They mean that all the potentialities this child has for being an ideal type of male are useless and that she has few potentialities for being an ideal type of female. It is considered legitimate to channel the child's development toward a masculine or feminine personality type, whereas, with less rigid traits of the potential, the child should be allowed to develop more freely. Two bad traits which are felt by adults to be present in the child at birth or shortly thereafter are the subject of vigilance on the part of the parents. These are cruelty and indifference to time. "Children tease unmercifully" is an example of a remark easily accepted by adults in the community, and these adults also make statements in reference to a child's disregard of time. It is the parent's responsibility to see that these two bad traits are under control by the time the child becomes an adult.

ACQUISITION OF THE POTENTIAL

The various features of the potential are felt to be largely inherited. Certain characteristics which are particularly thought to be acquired in this manner are: physical appearance and defects, some diseases, temperament and certain abilities. Sometimes traits are assigned to a specific progenitor, at other times they are felt to be reinforced through inheritance from a number of ancestors. Often traits are simply assigned to the father's or mother's side of the family.

A mother: "I don't know who Dick looks like. Dan is a Smith [husband's family] and Betty is a Smith. Clara looks just like me when I was a girl. I think Mary's a Smith too, she looks more like the Smiths."
Observer: "How about things other than looks?"
Mother: "The girls are all musical and that's nothing to do with me. The boys like music too, and I'm not that way at all. Grandma Smith is; she plays the organ over to the church in Westport. That is where the Smiths live."

Some other examples of inherited traits specifically mentioned by various parents included: physical defects—birthmarks, diabetic tendency, eyes out of line; disposition—temper, lowness, neatness, sensitiveness; skill—music, mathematics.

INFLUENCES ON THE DEVELOPMENT
OF THE POTENTIAL

In Orchard Town it is felt that the development of the potential can be influenced to some extent by a number of factors. First of all, the parents are considered to be important influences on the development of the child. However, other adults, the child's associates, and environmental factors are also thought to be important. In addition, development is thought to occur through a progression of stages. These stages influence the particular expression a child may give to his potential at any time. The stages are thought to be more or less inevitable and relatively inaccessible to influence.

A newborn infant, as an undeveloped potential, is very frequently viewed as a victim of his parents and elders who are in a better position than he to foresee the end product of his development. It is the duty of these elders to help the infant to realize the good aspects of his potential and to curb his bad aspects. There is relatively good agreement in the community on how to do this.

First, the parent is responsible for not doing anything which would prevent the child's natural unfolding in the future for the sake of personal convenience in the present. The parent should not impose his own standards upon the child any more than is necessary to curb his bad aspects until the child is old enough to evaluate parental standards in terms of his own nature. The statement is made in the church guide, "Enjoy your child; do not push him into development." The parent, ideally, acts as a kind of pleased observer who watches the child unfold.

Secondly, a parent is supposed to understand the child's potential insofar as this is possible. Irreparable damage is thought to occur if the child does not unfold his potentialities at the right time, so parents need to have some knowledge of norms. Norms are quite obvious after a child enters school, but even before this the parent is aware of how much the child is supposed to have accomplished at a certain age, either through the use of books as guides or through observing other children. If the child is not "normal" then it is the parent's duty to assist the child to reach the highest standard possible.

Spoiledness, laziness, nervousness, rebelliousness, discipline problems and lack of appetite are traits which in various degrees are thought to be emphasized by parental treatment of the child. Parents may try to explain these in other ways, but teachers and other members of the community feel the parent is at fault. Lack of discipline is thought to cause both spoiling and laziness, and forcing the child is thought to develop nervousness, rebelliousness, discipline problems and lack of appetite. The physical growth and health of the child are specifically parental responsibilities to the extent that it is a parental duty to see that the child has proper nourishment, avoids illnesses by dressing properly and keeps away from children with contagious diseases. It is also the parents' duty to divine and aid the development of the child's potential.

A mother: "I wish he would express a strong interest which is based on reality because I think that if you know what a child's main interest is you can feed into it right away. But I haven't located it and I don't want to impose one on him. He is quite verbal. I think children are born with the ability to spell or not to spell."

There is much evidence that the members of the community believe that traits may be acquired by members of the community through a shared physical and social environment. Numerous statements were recorded to the effect that the children or the adults of the town were of such and such a character. Here is an example of a statement by a teacher, who feels that this town in some way influences its children differently from other places:

The children in this town are not very demonstrative. The Polish children in the city are very respectful of their teacher. They will run from a distance to see their teacher. When I first came to this town I was teaching at the central school and as I was waiting for the bus I said "Good morning, boys and girls" to some children who were waiting for the bus and they just ignored me.

This belief in the ability to acquire traits from or be influenced by one's associates leads the parents to try to be good "models" for the child and to try to keep the child away from or teach him to evaluate bad models.

Education is felt as a very important influence on the development of the potential. Although a child may have a very desirable potential, no one believes it can be realized if the child does not acquire the requisite skills through education. As a means of education, the school is evaluated differently by different status groups in the community. The lower status parents feel that the town school is good, and a means of rising in the status hierarchy. Higher status parents often feel that the school in the town is actually inferior to home influence in educating their children.

The concept of stages has important influences on the child training system. There is a strong belief that a child goes through a series of stages which are common to all children or almost all children. The stages are considered to be almost, but not completely unalterable. Certain children, because of their nature, are thought not to go through certain stages, or, a clever parent is able to alter the effects of the stages. A mother says:

They all go through a whiny stage. When they are able to they go through a holding-on-to-mother's-skirts stage. Sam is at the stage where he doesn't want me to leave at night. He cries when his father leaves at night. Bill's in the cry-baby stage now. Don't they go through the same stages over and over?

At six they go through a stage of thinking nobody loves them. When Bill was six he didn't want any affection. He didn't want you to kiss him or anything, and now he likes to be loved.

Although the child may, at any stage, appear to be a particular type of person, this may be deceiving, since stages, by their nature, inevitably pass. The parent is asked to remember this. Making an issue of some bad trait may damage the potential with useless forcing, since the trait will disappear with the disappearance of the stage. Serious or criminal behavior, however, must never be ignored as "just a stage." It is to be noted that all stages are not bad. Good stages are sometimes taken as indicators of good potentials to which a child may eventually return after passing through a bad stage. Words used with reference to describing a stage through which a child was passing included: nervous, irritable, pleasant, happy, giving-away, imitative, can't concentrate, can't join in games, can learn about Jesus, can't mix sexes in learning, fascinated with babies, noisier, harder to handle, rebellious, and messy. At times, grade in school was used as the basis of definition of a stage.

CONSEQUENCES OF THE THEORY
ON PARENTS AND ELDERS

The fact that the child is viewed as a potential which the parents have the duty to assist in its development, and the related ideas about the potential, result in certain consequences for the emotional aspects of the parent-child relationship. If the child is viewed as a potential which the parents are supposed to develop, parents often react to having children as they would to having any responsibility. The emphasis on parental responsibility for the child in this community appears to be stronger than in other groups of our acquaintance. Here the responsibility for the child is focused on the two parents rather than spread over an extended family. Parents probably find it easier to take responsibility for a child whose potential is seen as similar to their own. For one thing, in terms of the view of the concealed nature of the child, this similarity of child-parent nature makes it easier for the parent to divine the concealed potential.

Sometimes, perhaps because of the concealed nature of the child's potential, parents in the community come to feel that they are victimizing their children. The parent is never quite certain whether or not he is doing his best for the child. Anxieties are alleviated by finding out what the child's potential is—insofar as this is possible.

The feeling of responsibility, if accompanied by a certain amount of lack of success in training a child, may lead parents to anxiety about their own adequacies which in turn leads them to force the child into certain channels of development. Since forcing is contrary to the belief system, this often leads to further anxiety. The ideas of stages, norms and the inheritance of characteristics act as convenient guide-posts to the parents and as comfortable explanations for the behavior of the child.

IDEAL CHILD FOR EACH AGE AND SEX GROUP

Although children with different potentials might be expected to behave differently, there are a certain number of characteristics which might be considered as ideal in a child of a particular age and sex. Some of the traits which were felt to be ideal are presented in summary form below. The data is not extensive on this subject. Unfortunately, no questions were asked which were directly related to it.

Ideal infant (both sexes): The ideal infant cries very little, and then only to indicate the pain of sticking pins. He has no physical defects, eats well, needs no entertainment. He goes happily to all adults. He has a nice odor about him (no odor of vomiting, feces, etc.) and is not ugly.

Ideal preschooler (male): This child is ideally aggressive in defending himself, but is not aggressive otherwise. He trains easily (bedtime, toilet, eating, etc.) and gets along with other children. He is not spoiled, or shy, or a show-off.

Ideal preschooler (female): She is not aggressive. She stands up for her rights only verbally. She, also, is not spoiled, shy, or a show-off. She trains easily and shows feminine tendencies like an interest in dolls, babies, etc. She likes to appear very helpful to her mother. However the female role is not quite as sharply defined as the male role at this age and during grade school. The female "tomboy" is censured less than the male "sissy."

Ideal school-age boy: A poem from the second-grade blackboard at school gives an idealistic prescription for the school-age child, both male and female:

> *Whole Duty of Children*
> A child should always say what's true,
> And speak when he is spoken to,
> And behave mannerly at table;
> At least as far as he is able.

This poem probably represents current adult standards of "company behavior" for their children and should not be taken too seriously as reflecting the actual expectations of the adults as to their children's daily behavior, although there is certainly some increase in parental standards when the children go to school.

A child of this age to be ideal must not be "sneaky"; he must appear alert. (This no doubt gives the impression that he has a high potential.) Although quiet is needed in the schoolroom, a too-quiet child is not admired either by parents or teachers. One statement relating to this was, "He was so quiet I didn't know who he was." Other similar remarks indicate that although teachers are constantly emphasizing orderliness and quiet, this is not entirely congruent with their picture of the ideal child. (A too submissive child gives evidence of a damaged potential, perhaps.)

An ideal school-age boy should be open, liked by both adults and peers. If he gets into troubles these must be of such a nature that they can be excused by the phrase "he is a typical boy." He should be willing to fight for his rights and be able to do so. He should also be willing to defend weaker children, not be a bully, and yet not be self-righteous, a tattle tale, etc.

Ideal school-age girl: This child, ideally should never engage in physical aggression. She should be alert, popular with boys and girls, not a scapegoat, and not rebellious. She should be neat, pretty or cute, get good marks in school, but not appear to be a "brain." Ideally she is shorter than most girls her age. She runs errands and helps mother willingly. She likes feminine games (dolls, etc.) and feminine frills.

DIFFERENTIAL STATUS OF AGE AND SEX GROUPS

There is no clear preference for any one age or sex group in comparison to others. This sort of preference seems to be idiosyncratic. It is probably due to factors peculiar to the individual's own childhood situation and not to any definite trend in the group. There are, however, a few opinions about age and sex factors. These will be discussed in this section.

Age

Adults vary on their preference for one age group or another. There seems to be a tendency for men to "be afraid of" infants and to prefer children with whom they can play. A number of women also reported that they did not care for the infant as much as for the child. One man reported that children's attitudes toward their parents changed after age six. Before that age, he said, children felt that parents were wonderful, and therefore he preferred the before-six age. This is probably not a feeling which is shared by any majority. At least one woman said she preferred older children because "they can take more care of themselves."

Children's looks are considered to deteriorate as they get out of the pre-school age, but children are rarely spoken of as liked or disliked on the basis of looks. At the same time as children take on the appearance of what is called "the awkward age" they are put into a kind of affective ice-box. Parents show less loving pleasure in their children as they grow older, but this is not to say that they do not like them.

The different stages or ages (insofar as these are congruent) are felt to have different contents. Some of the aspects of each of the ages may be liked while other aspects are disliked. The age which seems to produce the most anxiety in parents is that of early puberty. At this time the child has to cope more actively with his sexuality and from various reports he is rarely able to get the approval of his parents in this respect. In most families a barrier to free speech grows up at this time between parents and children. Parents have to relinquish a good deal of control over their children and they usually do so with anxiety.

Sex

Just as adult preference for an age group is an individual matter, preference as to the sex of the child varies. Remarks of a few parents suggest a tendency for fathers to want a boy and perhaps a slight tendency for women to want a girl. Two women who have only male children said they would have preferred girls before they had any children, but when they had boys they weren't disappointed. One said,

I always thought a little girl would be so much fun to dress, but I wouldn't change Tom [her youngest boy] for a million dollars; [calling the child's attention to the conversation] Would I, Tom? I asked Tom how much he loved me and he said "bigger than the whole world."

The second woman said that although she wanted a girl she wanted a boy for her husband's sake. Other women reported that they wanted a boy first or that they preferred boys. One woman who had three boys and one girl had a very strong preference for boys. She said that her one girl was more aggressive than all of her boys and that "(the girl) could knock all of the boys' heads together." The girl is not the oldest child in the family. Another woman felt that her husband "favors the girls" (they have one boy and two girls). The ideal family, perhaps, is considered to be one that has both sexes among its children.

Girls are described variously as "feminine," "not leaders," "never think of anything" (male peer speaking); while boys are people "you just can't insult," "bossy," "active," "real or typical boys," "the ones that really make trouble" (18–20-year-old boys). Boys should not be "effeminate," but girls may "play with boys as equals" without criticism, although the preference seems to be for girls who play the feminine role in the presence of boys. A speaker said to the "Ladies' Circle," "Boys can be so unpleasant parents lose patience with them." Perhaps all but the sexual aspects of child training are considered to be easier for the parent if the child is a girl. "A son is a son till he gets him a wife but a daughter's a daughter all of her life" is an opinion which is expressed often.

Most children, themselves, do not overtly express dissatisfaction with their sex whichever it may be. One girl said in a game, "I don't like to be men. I don't want to be a king. I want to be a queen or a princess." Sometimes there are aggressive feelings between the two sexes, especially envy of boys by girls. An older high school girl is very resentful of what she feels is a preference for boys in a school official. She says of him:

Everything is for the boys—nothing is for the girls. She then listed all the uniforms and equipment boys get and girls get "nothing!" He has made a rule that the girls have to have on gym suits everyday when they play games. This is "too cold in winter." The girls have resolved to practice hard and win first place in the area in athletics and then "if he doesn't praise us we're going to praise ourselves." The girls' gym teacher got very "brave" [in defending the girls] and got up in an assembly and told everyone how loyal the girls were about coming to cheer for the boys and how nobody came when the girls played a game.

Boys at times expressed resentment against older sisters, who had authority over them, but in general their resentment seemed less than that that of girls toward boys. Thus, while there is a conscious satisfaction in whichever sex role falls to one's lot, there is still a definite aggressive element in attitudes toward the opposite sex. Evidently the difference in the roles is sufficiently great to cause some jealousy about certain aspects of the opposite role.

SPECIAL STATUSES OF CHILDREN

A number of special statuses are found among the children in the town. The special statuses may be classified as: related to accidents of birth or conception and the inheritance of physical traits; related to the peculiar position of a child in the social system, such as sibling position or lack of true parents; and related to special types of training to which the child has been subjected. The special statuses are discussed below under these three headings.

Special Statuses Related to Accidents of Birth

A list of this class of statuses, taken from casual notes made throughout the year of fieldwork follows: slow or retarded children; twins; runts or children far below average in size; blue babies; deaf children; children born with heart ailments or under perilous conditions such as caesareans. Each of these statutes receive special treatment at times in the socialization process.

A child who is very much retarded mentally finds himself unable to keep up with his peers in school. If he is not too retarded he may be either kept back in school or put in slow groups in reading and arithmetic. If he is much retarded, he may be sent to a special school for retarded children or receive tutoring by people in the community who are paid to teach such children. If retardation is associated with personality or other difficulties the slow child is often the butt of teasing and ridicule by his peers and the exasperation of his parents and teachers. If he is just slow and does not stand out from the group as a disciplinary or social problem he may go more or less unnoticed, be shy, and remain as far as possible in the background of group activities. There were no seriously retarded children in our sample. If a child is merely below average in intelligence and his parents have no high aspirations for him there is generally very little problem. Parents do want their children to keep up with their age-grade in school and all parents in the sample who had children in danger of not-passing in school made special efforts to help them with their study. In one case at least this study took the child away from her peer group during informal play times.

A deaf child in the community associates freely with her peers. She is reported by adults to "use" her deafness at times to avoid hearing things she finds unpleasant. Thus, she represents a special discipline problem. She wears a hearing-aid and she is an expert lip-reader. So adeptly has the child managed her handicap that the observer would not have known of her deafness except for the visible hearing aid. She is not shy or withdrawn.

Children who are weak at birth receive special attention in their early months. This is almost inevitably true even when parents consciously try to avoid giving special attention to such a child. Such special attention is felt to be detrimental and to be likely to "spoil" children. Here is one mother's story of how she fed a child while she was paralyzed with the fear that he might die if he did not eat.

He didn't like the bottle too well; he didn't like to eat. I might have done it [started him drinking from a cup] to try something different to get some food into him. Because they told me if I could get enough food into him I might be able to keep him alive. They told me not to force him to eat, but I did. They told me he wasn't going to live anyway. He used to hold the food in his mouth and let it come out his nose so I used to hold his mouth and his nose and in order to breathe he had to swallow it. [The sequel to this is that the child is very much alive and leading a very normal life at present—age 5.]

A male child who is smaller than most children has a special status. One child's entire personality is considered by the people in the community to have been shaped by his small size. It is felt that he is constantly under pressure to prove himself physically to be as capable as other children, because of his small size.

Twins are generally welcomed. If one child is wanted, two are considered to be especially desirable. A woman who had twins reported her pleasure and her difficulties; these twins were in another special status, the first boys after three girls:

I don't know if the doctor said I wasn't going to have twins because he knew I didn't want them or not. I just thought it was awful hard to take care of them, and it is for the first six months; pretty hard for the first year; then it's not too bad.
They knew I was going to have twins after the first one was born . . . Poor George didn't know how I was going to feel about it. He was thrilled. Grandpa was more than thrilled because he had no grandsons and my sister was thrilled because she wanted a boy too—but two boys in the family!! . . . I wanted a boy so I was thrilled that it was a boy, and, after I got over the shock of it, it was a thrill to have two—one would have been spoiled. . . . It took the whole family to take care of them.

Twins, finding companionship in each other, are apparently less inclined to wander from home. These particular twins are likely to support each other in difficulty, act as consciences for each other, and probably to a greater extent than other siblings will tell their parents on each other.

Special Statuses Related to Position in the Social System

A list of some of these found in the community follows: only child, oldest child, youngest child, illegitimate child, adopted child, state child (boarding out with people in the town), children with a parent dead or missing, children of old age, step-children, children whose parents are employed as ministers, garbage collectors, teachers in the local system and possibly children of parents in a few other occupations.

Only children are considered to be in great danger of "spoiling." Although there were a number of only children in the community, only one was held up as an example of an only child. It was said of him by many people:

He is an only child and an only grandchild, and always had things other kids didn't have, like projectors, and he was always wanting to show them off, which frequently disrupted things much to the annoyance of the children. The children, also, don't like him very much.

A teacher said of another only child: "He is a show-off, being the only child. Usually whenever we have a visitor he starts showing off."

Parents as a general rule feel that they have been "stricter" with their first-born in all of his training than they are with following children. Youngest children, like only children are felt to be in danger of being "spoiled." Youngest children in large families often do have a financial advantage over more deprived older ones. The older ones grow up, get jobs, and buy things for young siblings which they were not able to have in their own youth.

Children born late in the life of the parent generally have a special status. Women reported enjoying their children more after they themselves had reached a more substantial age. A late child was at times embarrassing to one woman who, while enjoying him, found that in public places she often overheard people saying, "they must be his grandparents."

There were a number of cases of illegitimacy or suspected illegitimacy in the community. This was a fact which was mentioned in talking about a child, but there was no particular feeling against him. It was felt, however, that the unfortunate circumstances of his birth usually led to personality problems in the child himself. The child is not condemned, but parents of illegitimate children are not always so fortunate.

One child was adopted during the period of our stay in the town. If there were other adopted children, they were unknown to us. This child's parents were delighted to have him and were expected by the community to spoil him.

A number of "state" children board with various families in the town who receive remuneration for their care. At least one of these families keeps such children isolated from the other children of the town for fear parents would be worried that state children would be a bad influence. None of these families were interviewed. Some "state" children were reported to be nice children.

One family was observed casually who had one parent, a mother. The mother was considered to be trying to do a good job under very difficult conditions. The children were in a rather poor status position with regard to their peers, although they were well-behaved children by community standards. Adults "felt sorry" for the children. One man in the community sometimes invited the boy to go along with him and his son on outings, serving as a kind of substitute father. With special friends these children were well-received, but with the rougher element in the community they were the butt of teasing. Another family which had recently acquired a step-mother had children who were not considered to be good playmates by the more conservative and conforming members of the community. The children were also not popular with their peers.

A good many of the effects on the child of incomplete or substituted families, then, probably arises out of idiosyncratic factors in the personality of the individual child, and his lot varies accordingly. He has, however, "one strike against him" before he starts. People expect him to have problems.

Children whose parents have special occupations may have special statuses. Ministers' children are always gossiped about, condemned more for wrong-doing and praised more for good behavior than other children. As the minister's wife said, "No matter what we do we will be criticized." Ministers' families also cannot make the social distinctions in their social life that other community members make, so that their children must be indiscriminately exposed to good and bad influences. Garbage collectors' children are often taunted about their father's occupation by some children. Children of teachers are probably expected by their parents to be especially well-behaved in order to advertise the parent's worth as a teacher.

Special Statuses Related to Training

A partial list of these special statuses as given by parents is: problem child, whipping boy, stinker, hoodlum, and spoiled child.

An adult recalls that there were problem children in school with him.

. . . problem children . . . they were basically not interested . . . Baseball or fishing was the source of the turmoil . . . Some of them were not too bright . . . One did a lot of whittling around school . . . carved his initials on the banisters. Another slapped a teacher once . . .

Mothers often reported that their first child had always been a problem. Problem child in this sense meant difficult to socialize. A child who is spoken of as a problem is not generally thought of as an out and out delinquent. This idea usually does not even enter the picture, but occasionally it is felt that a problem child is in danger of becoming a delinquent. This would put him in a different status category. The cause of the problem child is generally felt to be the lack of experience of the mother in dealing with children or bad techniques in dealing with them. In these cases some kind of unpleasantness gets started between parents and child at an early age and tends to continue throughout life. It is so emotionally and unconsciously based, judging from reports, that it is seldom completely overcome. One woman reported that she had a much better relationship with her first-born son since he had been gone from home a greater part of each day to a nearby private school. Another woman said of her first-born daughter, "we have always gotten on each other's nerves." A father reported that a kind of submerged hostile battle was constantly going on between himself and his oldest son. These children were all felt to be problem children to a greater or less extent. None of them were considered to be "bad" or delinquent children.

One informant, on seeing a small boy, said, "There is a 'stinker,' a 'bugger.'" The observer asked what a bugger was, and got the following reply:

He's just mean as far as the rest of the kids go . . . He used to come by here and ring the door bell all the time . . . All the kids seem afraid of him. He rules everybody. He used to hit little Jonathan all the time.

Since this boy does not come from the type of family (which seems to be essential to and) which produces "hoodlums" he is only known as a "stinker."

Hoodlums may be considered to be such while not actually being, or they may be real hoodlums. "They (the children of a certain family) were considered hoodlums. Some didn't let their kids play with them. They weren't really hoodlums." Hoodlums are evidently members of lower-status families and of families who are reputed to neglect their children. Lower status alone is not sufficient to indicate that a particular child will be considered to be a hoodlum. If some children in such a family show signs of delinquency, the other children in the same family will generally be classed with the delinquent as a "hoodlum." Such a child is generally isolated as far as possible from the children of conforming families. He is generally found in association with other "hoodlums." Stinkers, on the other hand, are found in association with children of conforming families and are generally found in families which are not lowest in status.

For one reason or another, a child may become a special focus of the hostility of an adult. There is sometimes just such a child in a classroom. He may be particularly demanding of adults in general and used to having his way with them, or have characteristics which happen to strike a particular teacher unfavorably. Such a child may be called a "whipping boy" (or girl). The following incident is typical of the school experience of one such child.

After recess two boys had been fighting while waiting in line for the teacher to unlock the door, which had closed. The teacher sounded very angry about their fighting. One boy said, "I was already there and he tried to push me out of my place." Stanley [the whipping boy] said, "He punched me so I punched him." The teacher apparently decided on the basis of this brief questioning and previous experience that Stanley was at fault. She told him to put his head down on his desk for five minutes. "I don't want to see you."

✳
✳
✳

Chapter 12

Pregnancy and Childbirth

Most women of Orchard Town welcome the idea of having a child. There is some preference for the first child to be a boy, although there is also a definite sentiment for having a mixture of sexes among one's children. Moreover, boys are considered more difficult to control in childhood, and a mother with more than a couple of boys is the object of sympathetic concern.

However, while children are desired, pregnancy itself is regarded by some as uncomfortable and restrictive. Cravings for large amounts of strange foods are normally expected. A woman's legs sometimes swell. The appearance of pregnant women is widely regarded as awkward and embarrassing.

Women are supposed to be careful during pregnancy for the sake of the fetus. They should try to avoid any heavy physical exertion for fear of causing an abortion or miscarriage. Some women have a tendency to miscarry, and several women expressed worries about miscarriage. The doctor may prescribe hormone treatment and bed rest for threatened miscarriage. Pregnant women should also try to avoid exposure to contagious diseases and should remain in the best possible health. One mother reported that she stopped smoking when she was pregnant for the child's sake. The belief is often jokingly mentioned that if the mother is frightened by anything in pregnancy, the baby will show some mark of it. However, all regarded this as a superstition which no modern parent would take seriously.

While some indulgence of special food cravings is thought permissible, it is believed that pregnant women must control a tendency to overeat. The women have a general fear of becoming too fat anyway, and an excessive gain in weight is considered to be especially undesirable during pregnancy. If a pregnant woman eats too much, she will not only gain weight herself but her baby may be too large, and labor will be difficult. Nevertheless, both parents are proud of having a baby that is bigger than average.

Nowadays birth almost always takes place in a hospital in a nearby town, since there is none in Orchard Town itself. During our field work, one woman in town caused some raised eyebrows by her insistence that she wanted to give birth to her next baby at home. Her doctor said that this was the first home delivery he had had. But even a generation ago, home deliveries were not uncommon.

There is little danger of maternal mortality. If birth is difficult, an operation is resorted to. One woman in town had had three children by Caesarean operation without complications.

The women do not appear to enjoy their confinement at the hospital. The isolation and enforced rest annoy them. One mother complained of the attitude of some of the assistants at the hospital: "They carry the babies around like sacks of flour." A volunteer worker at the hospital felt that not enough attention was paid to the infants' crying.

Even after the mother returns home from the hospital she is considered somewhat weak and incapable of her full regular work. If possible, a grandmother or other relative may come to visit or a high school girl or an older woman may be hired on an hourly basis for a while to help out some with the housework.

There is no special ceremony at the time to celebrate the birth of a child or the return of the mother from the hospital. Both parents are

proud of the birth and receive congratulations from friends and relatives. The parents may send out cards announcing the birth.

✤
✤
✤

Chapter 13

Infancy

In the beginning of infancy the mother-child relationship is built
mainly around the question of care of the infant: feeding it and keeping it clean, warm, medicated, and out of harm's way. The infant is
considered to be especially susceptible to a number of dangers including contagious diseases, chilling, suffocation, and physical accidents, especially falling on its head.

Infants may be fed initially by bottle or breast. Ten out of our 24
sample children were nursed for a time by their mothers. The length
of nursing ranged from a few days to five months, at which time bottle
feeding was substituted. One child was said to have disliked bottle
feeding as a result of forcible weaning from the breast.

Some mothers said they simply could not nurse their babies, while
others expressed varying degrees of distaste or revulsion toward nursing. Even the mothers who did nurse their children usually worried
about whether they had enough milk. There is some indication that
mothers blame themselves for lack of milk and their inability to nurse.
Such a feeling of self-depreciation is reflected in the statement of one,
"I am not a good mother, and, of course, I will not be adequate to the
test of mothers—feeding my child." Most mothers who nursed were
not reluctant to wean their children from the breast, although one
mother who lacked enough milk to continue nursing her baby said
she "thought the world had come to an end" when she realized she
must stop.

A few years ago most children were on a feeding schedule. However,
recently "demand feeding" has become popular. In our sample all but
one of the children 5 years of age or younger at the time of the study

were reported to have been fed on demand, while all but two of the older children were said to have been fed on schedule.

Mothers have a wide variety of interpretations of the meaning of demand and scheduled feeding. Some mothers said they had scheduled feeding, yet reported they would vary as much as half an hour from the schedule. Other mothers would have considered this to be no schedule at all. These took pride in being "on the dot" in their feeding. They reported proudly that they adjusted their own activities to their schedule for the infant. The interpretation of demand, on the other hand, often was that the child was supposed to set up a schedule in his first few weeks after which the mother would follow the child's schedule faithfully, just as she would have followed a schedule she had set up herself.

One of the difficulties of full demand feeding is that it lets the infant develop the habit of waking in the middle of the night and crying for food. Most babies sometimes wake in the night anyway, and this is considered to be very trying for the mother and for the father as well if, as occasionally happens, he helps quiet the child. Feeding in the middle of the night is not easy if it involves heating a bottle and is not considered necessary for the child's development, and some mothers even look with disfavor on giving a baby a bottle to go to sleep on the grounds that he will become too attached to the bottle this way and weaning will be difficult.

The infant sleeps in a crib for a year or more. The crib is usually at first put in the parent's bedroom to facilitate care at night and to avoid disturbing any other members of the household. However, if space were available, most parents would probably prefer to put the baby in a separate bedroom of its own near theirs. It is not uncommon for parents to take the baby into their bed to quiet it, although most would try to put it back in its crib later and not let the baby sleep regularly with them.

Cleanliness is regarded as important, both for the baby's health and for its comfort. The babies wear diapers until toilet training is fairly well completed, and the diapers are changed frequently in theory and usually so in practice, although there may be some delay since the mother is usually busy with work around the house.

Infants are bathed daily although older children usually bathe less frequently. Some babies resent the bathing initially and cry, perhaps more from the restriction on their movement than anything. The baby's hands and face are washed several times a day, after and often before eating, and after playing with anything dirty.

Babies are generally kept clothed both for modesty and to keep the baby warm. We saw only one baby naked in the course of a year, and this one was having a bath. The babies at times seem to be over-clothed, although on hot days in the summer they may wear only diapers.

Adults consider it natural and largely inevitable for babies to cry a lot, although the crying is disliked and happy babies are admired. The mother's treatment of crying depends on her interpretation of what is bothering the baby. Often it is felt the baby is simply crying for com-panionship, as when the mother has been playing with it and leaves to do some housework. Indulgence of crying for companionship is felt to be bad, for it leads to a spoiled child. Moreover, letting the baby "cry it out" is good not only for its character but also may help exer-cise its lungs.

Babies are thought to cry frequently because of stomach pains due to either hunger or colic. A baby on demand feeding is fed when it cries and the mother thinks it is hungry. Very probably it will often get food to stop it from crying when it is not in fact hungry. A baby on scheduled feeding does not usually succeed in breaking its schedule by crying for food, but it may be given a rubber pacifier to suck on. If it is not too hungry or is really crying for other reasons anyway, the pacifier may distract it enough to stop the crying. Most babies are in fact quite fat and evidently get plenty to eat. One wonders how often Orchard Town babies really cry from hunger.

A baby may be thought to be crying from colic if it is known to have had plenty of food and rejects further food. A mother may treat this by "burping" the baby—putting it on her shoulder and patting its back. Colic is regarded as a problem for which there is no sure, rapid solution.

Constipation is also believed to be a common cause of crying by many mothers. The remedies for this are suppositories, enemas, and laxatives, although laxatives are perhaps passing out of favor.

Teething is thought to make babies cross and to lead to crying. Some parents feel that not too much can be done about this; others believe teething rings are effective.

Some babies cry at the appearance of strangers. Adults laugh at this, and the stranger will usually try to reassure the baby, often success-fully.

Chapter 14

Early Socialization

Although concern for meeting the physical needs of her baby domi-
nates the mother's early interaction with her child, a positive concern
with training and controlling the infant in certain respects emerges
at an early age.

As soon as the baby is "ready," the mother tries to replace the bottle
by the cup (if the mother has nursed her baby initially, the breast has
been replaced by the bottle before this). Mothers recognize various
signs of "readiness": when a child can hold a cup, when it can sit up
in a high chair, or when the child refuses the bottle or throws it away.
In any case most people feel uncomfortable to see a child feeding from
a bottle much after the time it begins to walk.

Supplementary food may be introduced a few weeks after birth.
This is generally orange juice, canned baby food, and cereal. At first
the mother feeds the baby with a spoon, but as soon as it is ready she,
at least in theory, encourages it to feed itself. Some mothers begin by
giving the child a spoon to hold and play with while the mother continues feeding him. When the child begins to pick up food with his
spoon, his hands are guided by the mother. Gradually the mother re-
leases her hold on the cup and the spoon, and the child is feeding
himself. An alternative method is to allow the child to begin to eat
with his fingers, leaving a spoon nearby so that the child may experi-
ment with using it. This last method enables independent feeding to
begin very early.

These methods may be considered as ideals. Quite a number of
mothers seem to be successful in carrying them out, although some find
them too much trouble. Among the mothers who do not tolerate the
"messy" eating stage, finger feeding is discouraged by staying with the
child, restraining his hands and pushing the spoon into his mouth
Even these mothers, however, recognize the other methods as ideal.

They say, "I know you are supposed to do it that way, but I just never could stand the mess." After the age of 2 the "messy" feeding period is passed, and most of the children are then allowed to feed themselves.

According to the mothers, most children were weaned gradually from the bottle as they learned to drink from a cup and to eat solid food. Eventually a point was reached where the baby tired of the bottle and threw it away repeatedly when offered. Few mothers reported any difficulties in this process. Those who did felt they were not serious and said something like "I guess he howled some."

Although mothers feel that feeding should be enjoyable and weaning an easy and enjoyable experience—they have read this and heard it at many times—it is nevertheless true that anxiety is noticeable in both of these activities. They may say, "It won't matter when he's 50, when he was weaned, who will know?" This suggests that it is a matter to be hidden if the child is slow in weaning. Even if the mother is able to resist the temptation to wean an older child forcibly, relatives may take over. The mother of one child in the sample went off for a brief vacation. Her sister and the child's father then told the child that there were no bottles left. Only three of the 24 children were reported to have still had a bottle at 2 years of age. A summary of the reported ages of weaning is given in the following table.

It can be seen that the majority of boys are weaned between 9 months and a year (8 out of 12). Half the girls were also weaned at this age, but 3 girls were said to have been weaned at 18 months.

	BOYS	GIRLS
5–6 months	1	1
9–10 months	3	3
1 year	5	3
1½ years	1	3
2 years	1	1
Over 2 years	1	

All weaning and feeding problems are felt to be the responsibility of the parents. Since the parents tend to blame themselves, and feel that others blame them in this area of training, guilt, anxiety, and feelings of inferiority are the concomitants.

As in other areas of training there is thought to be an ideal time to begin toilet training. However, different signs that the child is "ready" for training are used by different mothers. These may be sitting up, walking, understanding what the mother says, and so on.

The process of toilet training includes giving the child the "idea" by sitting him on a potty or toilet, grunting and running water, waiting for his "regular" time to put him on the toilet, or putting him on just after urination or defecation has occurred. In other words, the attempt is made to associate the process of urination and defecation with the toilet. The ideal is often expressed that in doing this, the mother should not force the child in any way. Forcing in toilet training is considered to be responsible for making a child rebellious; in addition, it makes toilet training difficult if not impossible.

In practice, mothers generally follow the ideal rules of toilet training when they have a child who is "easy to train." With a child who is difficult to train, the ideal is very distant from the real practice, and more severe measures are used.

We list below our impressions as to the frequency of certain toilet training techniques mentioned by mothers as occurring in the community:

Holding pot on lap and small baby on pot while feeding—rare

Putting on pot at regular times after child is able to sit up—frequent

Use of suppositories, soapsticks, or enemas at regular times—one fourth to one third of all mothers used these for bowel training

Spanking—occasional

Shaming—very frequent

Rubbing nose in feces—occasional

Praising for proper performance—very frequent

Taking up at night—frequent

Restriction of water after 4 or 5 P.M.—frequent

Promise of rewards for not wetting bed—frequent with bed wetting problems

As in feeding problems, parents also feel responsible about lack of success in toilet training. If the child was slow in learning, they felt that they had started toilet training either too late or too early. At other times they worried that they had been too strict. Mothers generally said that they were more "relaxed" with their later children, and in some cases the later children were more easily trained. Mothers do not, however, accept total responsibility for slow toilet training, since they believe that some children are just "naturally" (constitutionally) hard to train. They cite different children in the family who had similar treatment but varied greatly in ease of training.

The following table gives the mothers' rough memories on the time of completion of toilet training during the day. Most mothers noted the approximate nature of these answers.

It will be seen that the spread of ages for boys is much greater than for girls. Girls were trained more consistently at 2–2½.

	BOYS	GIRLS
11 months to 1 year	2	
1½ years	2	4
2–2½ years	3	8
3 years	1	
4 years	1	
5 years	1	
Over 5 years	2	

Mothers reported, however, that the age at which children were able to stay dry all night was much later. Four of the boys in the sample still wet occasionally. Two are 5, one is 7, and one is 10. Five of the girls still wet: three 4-year-olds, one 7-year-old, and one 8-year-old.

There is a suggestion in the data that if early toilet training is severe enough and consistent, it may be completed early in childhood regardless of constitutional factors. Mothers who took an early and strong stand on toilet training according to their reports succeeded in training the child at an early age. It was the mothers who wavered between leniency and strictness who tended to be least successful in toilet training.

Somewhere between two or three months to a year when the baby is thought to need less attention at night its crib is moved into another room. If it has an older sibling, the baby usually shares the sibling's room. The baby may still cry during the night and on such occasions be taken back into the parents' bed if it is not easily quieted.

Both parents, but especially the mother, are delighted by signs of physical and social maturity in the baby. Parents will compare their children as to the age when they learned to walk, talk, feed themselves, and so on and some even kept elaborate records in the form of "baby books." The mother talks to the baby from birth whenever she is doing things with it and encourages its laughing, gurgling, and foreshadowings of speech with smiles and words of praise. When the baby begins to talk, among its first words are "Mama," "Daddy," (or "Papa"), and "bye." At first the mother waves the baby's hand while saying "bye," but soon the baby learns to do both by himself.

A mother also may hold the baby while it practices walking. Much of the day the baby may be in a crib or playpen with sides of a convenient height for the baby to grasp and practice standing or walking.

At times the mother may stimulate motor activity by jiggling the baby on her knee or by other physical play. Some adults, especially men, may lift the baby over their heads or swing it around. The baby comes to like this eventually, and this sort of roughhousing continues in later childhood between men and boys, though not so long for girls.

The baby is given a number of toys which encourage motor activity, such as rattles, and later bouncing horses and wheeled toys which jingle or make other pleasant noises when pulled or pushed. Some of these are advertised as aiding the baby's physical development by encouraging exercise.

Although parents are annoyed by the baby's clumsiness and "racket," they believe that healthy, psychologically adjusted babies are noisy and active. Accordingly, the baby gets a certain amount of unintentional reward for being noisy and active, since the parents often show pleasure at these signs of good health (in turn presumably derived from good parental care).

As the baby grows and becomes more physically active, it comes into more contact with other people. There is less worry about exposing it to colds and other infectious diseases, although care would be taken to avoid visitors with an obvious severe cold. Women start taking the babies with them around town to friends' houses or on short shopping trips, and the mother also begins to leave the baby for short periods with friends, relatives, or occasionally paid baby-sitters. Nevertheless, the baby is with the mother more than anyone else and will generally cry for a while at the mother's departure.

The older baby's first contacts with new people are more with adults than with other children. If brought together with another baby of the same age the two would fight, it is thought. Older children may enjoy trying to amuse the baby if they happen to be confined with it, but in free situations they usually desert it for their own pastimes. We frequently observed a couple of fifth-grade girls wheeling some neighbors' babies, but they seemed to interact little with the babies and to be interested primarily in earning pocket money. If the baby has an older sibling, however, it will see this child around a fair amount of the time and probably sleep in the same room with it, even though the sibling may do little either for or to the baby. This lack of interaction with older siblings is reinforced by the parents since they generally discourage older siblings (unless quite markedly older) from assuming responsibility for infants on the grounds that the older child will be irresponsible and that it would also be imposing unduly on him or her. It is thought to be too trying for an older child to face the baby's antisocial behavior and maintain reasonable control over it.

A major problem is the baby's tendency to pick up any small loose object to play with, whether another child's toy or some possession of the parents'. Depending on the baby's age, the value and fragility of the object, and the importance of its owner, the mother may retrieve it forcibly, upon which the baby generally cries angrily, or wait until the baby abandons it in the hope of avoiding a "scene." If the latter, she will apologize to the owner that the baby "doesn't know any better." Older siblings do not always accept this apology calmly.

When frustrated in this or other ways, a baby may attack an adult physically by hitting, kicking, or biting. Biting is the most severely disapproved, and although expected, it is punished. Some mothers bite the child back; others say "No! No!," cry out in pain, or spank the child. If biting continues into childhood, as it had in the case of one 3-year-old, it is punished by neighbors not allowing their children to play with the offender.

Because of the ease with which the baby lapses into antisocial behavior, prolonged social life is not considered desirable for babies and is felt to tire them. Most of them spend a good part of each day alone in a crib or playpen or in a fenced-in yard. Children learn early in Orchard Town that interaction with others is spaced, separated by periods of withdrawal.

In addition to tiring the baby, it is believed that too much social attention can "spoil" him. Certain types of unpleasant behavior, interpreted by adults to mean that the infant wants social attention, are deliberately ignored. Crying is often one of these. The value here is inculcated that people are ready to share time with a pleasant person and are unwilling to spend time with an unpleasant one. Unpleasantness must be hidden from others by means of a social mask or, alternatively, one can withdraw from others.

Such contacts as the baby has with other human beings are not marked by close bodily contacts as in many societies. There are two opposing needs considered here—one the early need for warmth supplied by close bodily contact, and the other the pleasure in the free movement of limbs. In this society the second is highly satisfied at the expense of the first. Ample clothing also intervenes between mother and child. There are freedom and a certain privacy in this. These things continue to be valued in adult social life. At the same time there are often feelings that something desirable is missing from social relations. Perhaps what is missing is the satisfaction of the need for close contact with another human being.

✻
✻
✻

Chapter 15

Early Childhood

The period of early childhood begins when the child has learned to walk and talk effectively and lasts until he enters school in first grade. (There is no public kindergarten in town.) This time is felt to be the most important stage of character formation. Traits that are begun here are believed to carry through life. If the child does not receive certain basic training during the preschool period, training is thought to become much more difficult later.

Accordingly, the emphasis in the mother's behavior toward the child now shifts from care to training and control. The child no longer needs to be fed each spoonful of food, has learned to go to the toilet when appropriate (at least most of the time), and can walk around and get for himself toys or other things he wants. Even where he needs his mother's help, he can ask her promptly in words instead of simply crying and waiting for her to divine his wish.

RELATIONSHIP WITH FAMILY

The child's social relationships become less exclusive at this time. Within the family he has more to do with his father and older siblings when they are around the house, for he is now able to seek them out at will and talk with them. The father and siblings find the child more interesting at this age than in infancy and are more willing to spend some time with him.

Outside of the family the child is thought to be lonely if he does not have playmates of his own age. Children usually have a few such playmates living close by with whom they play regularly and freely during the day. However, the child of this age is still felt unable to meet the world in general independently, and he is therefore restricted to his immediate neighborhood.

TECHNIQUES OF DISCIPLINE

These children are highly aware that they have graduated from the rank of "baby" and are likely to exhibit considerable scorn of babies, whether a neighbor's child or a younger sibling. This feeling of superiority is the residue of the parents' praise for advanced behavior and their inciting the child by remarks like "Only *babies* do that. *You're* not a baby." The frequency of these remarks at this age, however, suggests that in adult minds, at least, there is concern lest the children lapse into babyish ways.

Proper discipline is felt to be especially important for a preschool child, and physical punishment is used more often in this period than at any other time. Initially children respond to the stronger discipline by temper tantrums. With these there is a shift in the parents' feelings toward the child from indulgence to some hostility toward his antisocial acts. Negatives become more common in the parents' speech with the child: "No! No!"

A typical mother shows some worry about others learning of the full extent of her troubles in controlling her child. In public she may tell him to stop doing something quite sweetly, addressing him as "dear," "darling," and so forth; when at home she might spank or speak more peremptorily for the same offense.

Because of the child's newly acquired mobility, it is no longer easy to confine him to safe parts of his environment, such as a playpen or crib. Moreover, narrow confinement would be considered undesirable for the child, since he is thought to need physical exercise and "space." Discipline which compels the child to observe restrictions on numerous acts well within his physical abilities becomes important not only for character molding but for the immediate control of the child.

SLEEPING ARRANGEMENTS AND
ATTITUDES TOWARD SLEEP

Children of this age have already been moved out of the parents' room for sleeping. However, it is not unusual for small children to crawl in bed with their parents during the night or in the early morning. In any case, parents are careful not to allow their young children to see them having intercourse. One woman reported that when she was a child she would—over her mother's objections—get in bed at times with her older brother for warmth and comfort. Presumably some of the current generation of children do this same thing, but we did not inquire as to frequency. Apart from questions of impropriety, parents would feel that the children would interfere with each other's sleep by sleeping in the same bed or even in the same room.

Most preschool children, however, sleep in a bedroom containing two beds, twin or bunk. Of the 10 children of preschool age in the sample, 6 sleep in the same room with siblings of the same sex, 3 with siblings of different sex, and 1 sleeps in a room alone, for he has no siblings living at home. There is some feeling that ideally children of opposite sex ought to have different rooms even at this age, but this is not considered important enough to warrant buying or building a new house if the present house is not big enough. Children change into special sleeping garments before they go to bed for the night. The most usual garment for both boys and girls is a pair of warm pajamas, although little girls may at times sleep in nightgowns.

Parents believe it is important for children of any age to get plenty of sleep in order to "grow." If left to themselves, children, it is thought, would not get enough sleep and would try to stay up as late as older people. This would be bad for their health and make them cross and hard to manage. Preschool children are accordingly put to bed at an early hour in the evening and are allowed to sleep as late as they will in the morning. One suspects also that a desire to have the children out of the way in order to free time for the parents to engage in their own activities is a stronger motive in putting children to bed early than many would like to admit.

Many children resist being put to sleep. When siblings sleep in the same room, they often whisper to each other regularly for half an hour or more and get into arguments as to who is keeping whom awake. Children also think of various excuses to get out of bed (e.g., go to the toilet) or call their mother (e.g., get a drink of water). One mother, who put her children to bed right after supper, regularly camped at the head of the stairs every night until the children had calmed down.

Many preschool children take a nap in the afternoon or are at least put in a room for a nap and expected to remain lying in bed reasonably quiet for an hour or so. Mothers often took naps at the same time. Some children object to taking naps, especially if they know one of their friends does not have to. However, the afternoon nap does not seem to be as much a focus of mother-child struggle as evening bedtime. Most children stop taking regular naps before they enter first grade.

MORNING ROUTINE

In the morning, preschool children have considerable freedom as to when they will get up. Most of them are neither required to get up by a certain time nor required to stay in bed until a certain time. Rising times were reported as varying from 6 A.M. to 9:30 A.M. If children are in the habit of getting up before their parents do, especially on weekends, they are taught early in this period to play quietly in parts of the house where they will not disturb their sleeping parents.

In some families, the father leaves early in the morning for work and often does not see his young children before leaving. In families where the father gets up early, however, children are more likely to go to bed earlier and therefore may be up in time to see father briefly before he starts off for work. It may be that rising time has grown later in North Village in the last half century and that formerly children were forced to get up early in the morning for breakfast.

Some preschool children dress before and some immediately after breakfast. If they are confined to the house because of recent illness, or even bad weather, in some families they may stay in their night clothes all or part of the day. But it is felt improper for a well child to remain in sleeping clothes much after breakfast on an average day.

CLOTHING AND DRESSING

The typical preschool dress is shirt, blue jeans or trousers, underwear, and sneakers or rubber-soled shoes. On hot summer days some children, mostly girls, wear shorts rather than long trousers. Short-sleeved shirts are also more common in the summer, and at this time boys, but almost never girls, may go around in the neighborhood without a shirt. Shoes are worn outside at all times. In the winter the children may put on a sweater over their shirt if the house is drafty and must put on extra outdoor clothing to go outside. On cold days they are expected to put on a snowsuit or a heavy jacket and snow pants and rubber overshoes if the ground is covered with snow or is muddy.

In general, children wear the same clothing throughout the day, but all of them have dress-up clothes for special occasions. On these occasions the little girls may appear in stiff petticoats and dresses, patent leather shoes, frilly hats, and even white gloves and a small purse, while the boys are more likely to have a white cotton shirt in place of the usual colored or patterned one, leather shoes in place of the usual sneakers, and a small jacket which matches their trousers. Miniature ties for boys are also worn occasionally.

There is much variation among young children as to how much they dress themselves. Even the most competent may require their mother's help with a few troublesome items, such as socks, shoestrings or buckles, and shirts with tight necks. Some mothers try to get their children to dress themselves as soon as possible in order to relieve the mother of this chore. Other mothers like to help the child, and still others are not satisfied with the way the child gets his own clothes on. Apart from the mother's attitude, mothers mentioned that children with an older sibling would often learn from the latter when much parental instruction had been seemingly fruitless. Moreover, all mothers appeared to give lip service at least that the child should learn to dress himself when he showed himself ready.

Of the children in our sample, some liked to dress themselves and resented help from the mother. Others asked for or were pleased to have the mother's help. If, as often happened, a child was dawdling with his dressing and the mother wanted to take him someplace, she would often take over and do it for him. Some remarks made by the mothers about the children dressing themselves follow:

I didn't set any time, I just waited until she wanted to do it. I was trying to teach her to tie at a time when I thought she should know but she didn't learn it even though I worked and worked, and then about a year later she started doing it. I found that true with her in almost everything.

I guess I did get him to dress himself by the time to go to school, but the other boobs I had to dress. On tying shoes his younger sister did it before he did and he finally got shamed into it, although he could have done it if he'd wanted to bother.

I dressed him longer than you should dress a child. As you can see, he's been babied. When he started I just helped and then I'd say, "Let's see you go; see if you can be a big man," and then I'd help him. He could do it by himself, but I like to help him.

She can dress herself, but I don't let her if I can help it. She gets everything on backwards.

Among the boys in the sample, the earliest reported time of starting to dress oneself was 1½ to 2 years of age. The latest age for completing taking over this responsibility was 6. Girls, in general, started dressing themselves a little earlier and took over the responsibility completely sooner than did boys. Four girls were reported as starting to dress themselves at 2 to 2½ years. In any case, it is considered that children should be able to dress themselves by the time they start to school, and this ideal is usually achieved in plenty of time for most items of clothing.

MODESTY

Apart from the problem of getting clothes on the children, there is the further problem of keeping them on. At this age the children themselves are aware of the rules for modesty but lack enough motivation to observe them at all times. On hot summer days or in the warmth of the well-heated homes, the young children are tempted to remove all or some of their clothes. Besides the desire for physical comfort there is a fair amount of conscious exhibitionism, which the children try to conceal from adults, not always successfully. One boy aged 4 was observed showing his penis to a girl about the same age, and both were giggling. At this particular time they did not happen to be caught. One mother told proudly how her son had reported similar acts by his friends (he himself disapproving), while another mother merely commented, "Oh, all boys have to do that." Another mother reported that she had had to speak a couple of times to her two daughters, aged 4 and 7, who had turned upside down in front of their older brother, aged 12.

Most parents do not react so strongly to the child exposing himself at home among the family, but improper exposure by children outside the home is something parents appear to be very much concerned with, although they also subscribe to the belief that one "should not make an issue of modesty." We would conclude that in this area ideal and actual behavior are widely separated.

For instance, one mother who reported that she never made an issue of modesty told how she had made her daughter, when small, walk down the street naked in punishment for taking her clothes off outside repeatedly. One case was recorded of a mother keeping a 3-year-old girl in the house for a week as punishment for undressing outside. Almost all parents said that although they were not concerned with modesty, their neighbors were.

Within the home most (but not all) parents take reasonable precautions so that their children do not see them naked. Locks are always found on bathroom doors and are frequently used. However, they try not to make an issue of this also. They feel that the last generation of parents was too strict. This generation of parents feels that they have the "casual" approach.

My mother and father were the type who never let their children see them without their clothes on, and they wouldn't so much as kiss each other on the mouth in front of us—no demonstrativeness. I'm not that extreme. I believe that if your children come into the room and you are putting your clothes on that you should go on about it casually and not make an issue of it. That way they don't think anything about it. My children take it as a casual thing.

MEALS AND DIET

When the preschool child comes to breakfast in the morning, mother is generally in the kitchen, father has left for work, and, if he has older brothers or sisters, they have usually already left for school. Very few families eat their breakfasts together. Some preschoolers often get their own breakfast if it is simple enough (toast or dry cereal). Mothers want their children to have "balanced diets," but breakfast alone does not have to include all the necessary food elements. One mother said she did not worry about what her child ate for breakfast so long as she drank her orange juice and milk.

Children and other members of the family all get three meals a day and generally eat them on schedule, although schedules vary somewhat from family to family. In contrast to breakfast, lunch is almost always eaten together, except that the father is usually absent. The evening dinner is the most elaborate meal except on Sundays, when the noon meal may be larger.

Standards for table manners vary from family to family, but all families have some behavior on which they insist. These apply especially to the evening meal when the whole family is together. Proper table manners are seen as making the child more acceptable socially. This is clearly illustrated by one mother.

I don't often praise them but when children are here who don't have good table manners, I'll say, "Now, you see, you don't like that. Now you know what other people think when you go out in public and don't eat right."

Some of the activities which are socially unacceptable at the table are listed by this mother.

Now I have been beginning to give her a little salad, which is all tossed, and I let her pick out the onion. I say, "Well, just put it to one side and don't speak about it. I'll beat the brains out of the next one that makes one of those disgusting noises" [laughing]. I try to keep control over the conversation. Of course, they do forget. . . . I feel that I should give way a little bit, but I don't because I feel that if they're going to sit at the table with us I have to insist for my sake. Now my son is the one who will drop food onto the table. My daughter doesn't. She doesn't like to have to chew up meat either. . . . I have told her that things don't look nice and I suppose I make a face. . . . I think they do want to imitate too, don't you know, and they do like to go out occasionally too, and I'll say, "Well, I don't see how you expect us to take you out to a restaurant if you can't do so and so. . . ." I just ask her to do it. I don't have to get after her too much. And, of course, I do overlook. If it's something like putting her arms up in the air, and I just wanta break her of the habit I poke her and whisper at her and that's partly so that my son won't make any remarks, because he's highly scornful in his way with her. So I make believe I'm her pal in telling her so he won't. Just like if you whisper in nursery school the kids will shut up."

Most children are subject to considerable pressure from their parents to eat a "balanced diet" at meals. Children may be required to eat certain foods considered especially critical nutritionally, such as milk, meat, and vegetables. Some families have the rule that a child must at least taste everything on his plate. One family was reported to let the child eat what he pleased every day of the week, but on Sunday he was required to "clean his plate." Parents also try to get children to eat by persuasion, telling them how good the food tastes or how much it will do for them. "Carrots make your hair curly" was heard from one grandmother, although most mothers would probably try to be more "scientific" than this and say something about vitamins, minerals, and proteins.

Some mothers forbid eating between meals, but more allowed snacks now and then. One child in the sample seemed free to climb up and get food from shelves or take it from the refrigerator whenever he chose. One mother was never heard to refuse food to her children whenever they asked. However, many mothers try to limit the amount of food a child has between meals in order to get him to eat his meals.

Families differed greatly on giving sweets to children, although nearly every child was reported to have a "sweet tooth" and was subject to some restrictions as to quantity and occasion. Parents believe that eating too many sweet things tends to produce tooth decay, destroys the appetite for more wholesome foods, and may lead to an undesired obesity. There are generally restrictions on eating candy, cookies, or ice cream immediately before meals, and permission for eating them after meals may depend on eating certain required foods at mealtime. Some mothers never brought a sweet into the house so as not to tempt the child with them. In some families it was taboo for the observer to give either gum or lollypops to children, while in others it was allowed as a special treat, and in still others the mother trusted the observer's discretion.

One of the latter mothers always had a large supply of lollypops and ice cream, and her children were in general indifferent to these. This was the mother mentioned above who was never seen to refuse her children food. Although she was exceptional in her methods, we have no reason to suspect that she disagreed with the general view that children should not eat too many sweets. Perhaps she could be so permissive partly because her children had not developed a craving for sweets.

All children, even those given considerable freedom in between-meal snacks, are taught not to ask for food at neighbors' houses. One mother said with pride that she knew she could trust her daughter not to ask for something even though she might want it very much. Even the ceremonial begging which takes place at Halloween called "Trick or Treat" make some parents nervous. Some parents, especially those who try to restrict eating between meals, are angry if a neighbor offers a child food. Neighbors who do give food to others' children try to ascertain in advance how the mother feels about this and follow her wishes. The neighbor may also check apologetically with the mother later to make sure she has not done wrong.

TOILET TRAINING

Toilet training is generally well under way by late infancy, but certain refinements continue to be taught into the preschool period. Many children of this age wet their pants from time to time. Punishment for such a slip is often severe. Younger preschool children may call their mothers to wipe their bottoms after defecating, although they normally learn to do this themselves before entering school. They are also taught during this period to close the door when they go to the toilet, flush it after they are finished, and wash their hands. When a child goes to the bathroom, the mother often listens for the noise of the toilet and faucet. If she does not hear them, she reminds the child, who generally obeys without too much fuss. Constipation and irregularity in defecation (ideally once a day after breakfast) continue to be regarded as a problem with some children. Anal suppositories and enemas may continue to be used, but the mere threat of them is more frequent than actual use, and this is often sufficient to "inspire" the child to defecate.

RELATIONSHIP TO MOTHER

The preschool child continues to spend most of his time under the supervision of his mother in some sense, although some of this supervision is rather nominal, as when the mother is busy with housework and the child playing outside in his own or a close neighbor's yard.

Some children spend much of their time during the day tagging along after their mothers around the house. Mothers vary in their reaction to this. Some mothers say they cannot work if a child is anywhere near them. Others like having the child ironing nearby on a toy ironing board as the weekly ironing is being done or having a small boy on a chair beside them deciding for the mother what kind of a "fence" to put around a pie.

All children see enough of their mothers at work to learn how to do some simple tasks, and from time to time they ask to be allowed to do these. The mother is often too busy and refuses, but if the task is not dangerous, and if she is not too pressed for time, she may let the child take over. Most such work is considered to be more for the child's amusement and for the long-run value of his character than for any immediate practical value. Speed and perfection are not expected. One mother said:

> You give them something to do. If it's something new you don't know how well they're capable of doing it. If they get it done you know they tried. That goes with the child. Some child might get it done quicker and well. You can't criticize the child who tries and doesn't do it as well, if they've tried as hard.

CHORES

Children of this age are at times required to do a few chores, however. They are expected to pick up their toys at times, although not without prompting. If the mother is in a hurry with her housework, she may send the child to fetch things elsewhere around the house. Some children are asked to take their dishes off the table. A child who would regularly do these or other chores without reminders is unimaginable to Orchard Town mothers. There is, moreover, no rule that a child must do any chore regularly and unfailingly. Mothers say, "I'm afraid I feel that the important thing is to know they can do it." However, if a child refuses to do small chores like this when requested, he will be scolded, and punishment or threats are often applied, although it is thought desirable to avoid these if possible. With toys to be picked up, for instance, either parent may threaten to throw them away if the child leaves them there.

Even though children do little "work" themselves, they soon learn a sharp distinction between work and play, or being busy and free, by observing their mothers and other adults. And they can see the contrast between the tense face of a mother who has gone through a stretch of housework and child care, and the vivacious face of one who has been attending a club meeting with her friends. From such observations and from casual remarks the child learns that much work is considered unpleasant by adults. The mother's irregularity and reluctance in assigning her children chores probably communicate the same lesson in a different way.

INDOOR ACTIVITIES

Young children have a number of unsupervised indoor activities in which they may engage by themselves while their mother is "busy" at various times between breakfast and evening meal. They may play indoors for limited periods when the weather is good or all day when it is bad. When playing indoors they sometimes play by themselves and sometimes with one or two children of close neighbors. However, mothers usually do not allow groups of more than two or three children to play together indoors, for they are considered to be too noisy and hard to control.

GAMES

Some young children are fond of playing various purchased board games when the weather is bad. In these the players move counters along toward the goal on the basis of some chance mechanism. We saw some very simplified board games which children of the age of 4 and up seemed to understand sufficiently to play. Small children play these sometimes with their friends and other times with older members of their family.

Drawing is a common indoor activity. Children start scribbling on paper at a rather early age. They are left alone with crayons and pencils as soon as they have learned not to draw on the walls or furniture. Children enjoy coloring books, which their parents may buy for them. In Sunday School children regard coloring and drawing as activities which are more enjoyable than the regular educational activities. Parents generally react to the children's drawings with indiscriminate praise and amusement. Coloring books in which children fill in outline pictures with crayons are especially popular.

TOYS

Children of Orchard Town, like most American children, have a large number of toys to play with. There are certain toys or playthings which it is felt that all children should have and which, in fact, nearly all children do have. There are others which only a few children have. In the opinion of the majority of adults in the community, children with many more toys than average are "spoiled" or in danger of being spoiled.

Many of the toys are used indoors part or all of the time. Most important are blocks, artificial stuffed animals, miniature trucks and cars. For girls, dolls and accessories are important, while for boys, toy pistols and guns are very popular, and toy soldiers and accessories are also fairly common. Girls also often want toy pistols and borrow them from boys, although parents hesitate to give girls this sort of thing. Most people agree that boys should not play with true (human) dolls, although stuffed animals are regarded as suitable toys for small boys. As soon as children learn to walk they are given variously shaped toys with wheels to pull around or push. These are perhaps more toys of late infancy than early childhood. Older preschool children do not play with these "walking" toys much.

Toy musical instruments are a fairly common sort of toy but are rarely used as practice instruments for learning how to play adult musical instruments. Their main significance is as noise makers, often to the annoyance of the parents who originally presented them to their children.

Young children, particularly, often break their toys, and this is a source of chagrin to the parents. Breakage is punished only verbally, usually with such remarks as "You won't get another one."

PETS

Most of the children in our sample had pets of some sort. About half had dogs, and somewhat fewer had cats. Two families had horses, and the children of these families were popular with the other children for this as well as other reasons. The children of neighbors enjoyed watching the horses even when they did not ride on them. Some families had lesser forms of pets, such as rabbits, hamsters, parakeets, canaries, goldfish, and tropical fish.

Dogs and cats are the objects alternately of rough affection and wrath from young children. It is considered important to train children not to abuse them. Children are taught early not to anger dogs, and adults try to restrain pets to protect both the children and the animals. People express pity for animals who are subjected to the pummeling of young children. Most of these household pets have gentle natures, in contrast to the aggressive and hungry dogs found in many societies. One child in the community had maltreated his pet dog, which died as a result. This child was criticized bitterly, and the criticism was recollected and renewed when the child was given a new dog a few years later.

TELEVISION

One important indoor activity, which is new with this generation of children, is watching television. Many children in the sample spent much time each morning watching "Ding Dong School" at 10:00 A.M., and "Big Brother" at 12:15. One boy, aged 4, regularly joined Big Brother in his daily salute to the flag and toast to President Eisenhower with a glass of milk. He became very angry with his mother if his milk was not on hand for the occasion. Some children answered questions Miss Frances asked them on "Ding Dong School" as though they could really talk to her. This was a source of some learning, especially of etiquette.

Parents had not made up their minds how they felt about television. Some thought their children progressed rapidly in understanding and speaking because of it. An older woman criticized, "When I was young we made our own good time; now the children sit glued to television." Most parents of preschool children, however, allowed them considerable freedom in watching television during the daytime. In general, when they were allowed indoors, they were allowed to watch television, although they were encouraged to spend much time outdoors in acceptable weather.

OUTSIDE PLAY

Parents encourage their children to play outside in the yard as much as possible except in wet or very cold weather. There is somewhat less freedom about going outside in winter because it is necessary to put on warm clothes. The parents want the children outside for their health, as they say, for the "fresh air and sunshine" *and also* for "peace and quiet" in the house. Orchard Town parents especially urge their children to play outside, and perhaps the community attracts residents who want this for their children. Except for infants, play in the yard is not usually supervised by an adult. However, for children of preschool age there is always an adult in the house, usually the mother. Even small children may be put out in the yard to play in good weather while the mother goes about her work inside, listening for the child's cry.

The area in which the child is free to move at will increases gradually as he grows older. For a child to the age of 3 or 4, this may be only a few yards adjoining his own yard. Playing away from home is somewhat controlled by the environment. Some children live in more dangerous environments than others. Also, some children live great distances from places where they might play with other children. Most of the 4-year-olds are allowed to go across a quiet street to play. Until they go to school, however, most children stay at home or in neighbors' yards to play. One 4-year-old girl goes to the store, across a busy street, about two blocks from home. She seems to be entirely reliable and capable. Crossing streets which have been forbidden, playing with knives and matches, and going long distances from home without permission are all severely punished.

PLAYMATES

When preschool children play outside, they are most commonly playing with one or a few other young children. During school hours their playmates are necessarily of about the same age, but during vacation or after school they often tag along after the younger schoolchildren, who condescend to pay them some attention if they are not too busy.

Nearly all young children have tricycles, and many also have wagons and scooters. The tricycles, which are very popular, are invariably called "bikes" by their owners and often by older children and adults. However, true two-wheeled bicycles are not generally obtained until the child reaches school age. Preschool children spend much of their time "going places" with their tricycles or wagons, although these places are within a strictly delimited area close to the home.

Preschool children either have a sandbox or sandpile of their own or have access to one in a neighbor's yard and spend much time making roads, bridges, and tunnels, over and through which they run toy trucks and cars. At other times they also mold the sand into animal figures, houses, "cupcakes," and so on. For these purposes they use either special toy shovels, buckets, and molds or various kitchen utensils.

In their play in the sandbox, children get into arguments from time to time over the use of toys. These arguments are nearly always about taking turns, not about ownership. The children know remarkably well who owns which toy. They will remember ownership of new-found toys which have been lost in the bushes for months. The arguments sometimes degenerate into fights, but any loud screaming usually brings out the mother in whose yard the children are playing. Mothers encourage their children to share their toys and be generous, but they also encourage proper care of toys and respect for the property rights of other children. At the end of the day major toys should be returned to the owner's home.

THEFT

The children's attitudes toward each other's toys reflect the general respect for property rights which parents strive to instill in them. Taking something belonging to another, even as a teasing gesture, usually brings a reprimand from the parents if they see it, and intentional theft brings more severe punishment. A typical punishment would be for the parent to accompany the culprit in returning the stolen goods to the owner with an apology. In one instance the mother of the culprit in addition prohibited her child from visiting the owner's house again. Children who have a reputation for thievery are also watched carefully by former victims, who usually discourage or prevent them from entering their houses more than other children.

In spite of punishments and reprimands, there is a considerable amount of petty theft by some children in the community. Some children, preschool and older, are given to theft of small amounts of candy from the local stores. Some adults feel that preschool children should not be punished too severely for occasional thefts of this sort, for it is considered that they "do not understand yet." Theft between children, as distinguished from "borrowing without request," appears to be considerably rarer than theft from adults and is controlled by the children themselves as well as by parents.

Preschool children, especially the younger ones, play few if any formal organized games with each other of the sort which school-age children play. The boys, however, tag along with the older children playing "Cowboys" and shoot their toy pistols imitatively. Young boys, but not girls, do a fair amount of playful wrestling with each other, an activity which continues on into school age.

PLAY GROUPS AND FRIENDS

In general, children of this age play with whatever other young children live close to them. There is some split by sex when enough playmates are available, but there is little restriction according to status differences of parents. However, children give signs of being aware of status differences at an early age. We noticed that one boy, aged 4, identified the make of a large number of cars, which are important symbols of status. He was also concerned about which cars are better and repeatedly informed the ethnographers, "Our Oldsmobile can crash your old Nash."

Although mothers are little concerned about the social prestige of the families of the young children's playmates, they do not consider all playmates equally desirable. But the discrimination is primarily along the lines of character and manners rather than wealth or prestige of parents, although wealth and prestige do influence adult relationships. A "fresh," "sneaky," or "cynical" playmate is a "bad influence" which might affect the child's character unfavorably if he associated too much with such a friend. Mothers do not as a rule overtly forbid all contact with "bad influences," but discourage them.

Well, there have been a lot of friends. I don't believe you should say, "You can't play with this one and you can't play with that one." That sort of drives them to it. I have told them why I don't like certain children. There are a few around here, I didn't say she can't play with them. I don't like them around. Now I like to have her play with Sue. They seem to get along good together. . . . Meg's [a sneaky child] the one I really would rather she didn't play with. I don't tell her that, I just don't want Meg in my house again. If they play they can play outside. I don't care too much for the Roe kids, but they don't come here often.

Some mothers who find that their children are playing too much with "bad influences" arrange at times to have the children pay visits to "good influences" in friends' homes.

Parents want their children to be popular with their playmates and not be bullies, but they also want them to "stand up for their rights" enough so they will not be mistreated. Parents allow more antisocial behavior toward children they do not approve of. A child who was unpopular with adults was observed being excluded from a game of tag by an older boy. The parent of the older boy was present and ignored this. This was incongruent with this parent's stated values. The unpopularity of the victim was evidently the parent's reason for ignoring the act.

Young children are apt to demand their own way when playing with children their own age. Mothers said that they do not interfere under these circumstances unless someone gets hurt or angry. However, they urge children to "take turns" having their own way with each other. They also point out repeatedly that other children will not like them if they are "bossy" or do not let other children "have a turn." When someone goes home angry, one mother says, "I don't blame them, when are you gonna learn to take turns?" Mothers are proud if their children are "able to be bossy without antagonizing friends."

SPECIAL ACTIVITIES

The preschool child's daily routine of informal, unsupervised play is interrupted at times by special activities with the mother or, on weekends and in vacation, with other members of the family. When the mother goes to buy groceries or on other errands, she generally takes her young child along if there is no one at home to baby-sit.

It is customary for women with young children to visit each other. These visits and similar visits to the child's home by other women provide an occasion for training the child in certain elements of etiquette. Children are instructed to make a little polite conversation with the members of the family whom they visit and especially to thank them for the "nice time" on leaving. Punishment for bad manners is not lacking. A child who broke wind when one of us was present was instructed to apologize and leave the room immediately and to go to the toilet. The same child had a piece of gum taken away from her when she forgot to say "thank you." Preschool children taken along at these times are expected to play more or less by themselves and not interrupt adult conversation or activities. If possible, children should leave the room when adults want to talk to each other; this is partly to avoid interruptions. Some mothers excused short interruptions on the ground that children forget what they are going to say so quickly.

Besides these visits and errands where the child is an appendage to an adult there are some special recreational excursions more specifically for the child's entertainment. Parents may take young children to museums, zoos, the circus when it visits a nearby city, to the movies, or other shows in the city. During the summer many children spend much time swimming in the local ponds. Here they are usually under nominal adult supervision, that is, an adult is in sight, will tell them not to go out too far in the water, to come out if they seem to be getting cold, but otherwise will do little in the way of supervision of specific activity. Mothers are responsible for most of these recreational excursions, but the father may also be involved on weekends or during his vacation.

RELATIONSHIP TO SIBLINGS

In the middle afternoon, after a nap if any, older brothers and sisters and other older neighborhood children come home from school. Some older siblings are old enough for the mother to leave in charge of the preschool child while she goes on an errand. Children under 12 are not considered capable of having complete charge of a small child. Five or 6 years age difference is not considered to be enough to make an older sibling a good disciplinarian. However, such siblings are often left in charge of younger brothers and sisters for short periods with varying expectations. The mother will direct the older child "to correct, but not to punish"; "to watch and protect but not to punish; I'll take care of that when I get home." One mother gives stronger authority to the oldest sibling, "If she is put in charge the younger child is told she must mind her." A 12-year-old boy, who is often left in charge of three younger sisters, is said by his mother to be "an old crab and demands more than necessary when sitting . . . the kids resent it if it's unreasonable."

Older children are expected to report on dangerous undertakings or major disobediences of their younger brothers and sisters, but they must be careful not to "tell on" them too much. With less serious offenses, the parents are more liable to reprimand the tale bearer rather than the offender. Older children are not usually allowed to hit or hurt a younger one unless the younger one "asks for it." Asking for it consists of prolonged teasing or using a valued possession of an older sibling without permission. The general attitude here is stated by one mother, who says:

> Jeffrey [3 years old] sometimes slams little Raymond one. Last night they were sitting at the table and Raymond did something Jeffrey didn't like and Jeffrey hit him. I'm always saying to him, "You're not his mother; you leave him alone. I'll punish him."

Brothers and sisters who are only a couple of years apart are felt to have important relations which affect the development of each. They may amuse, teach, encourage, or "tattle" on each other. Two brothers, three years apart, amuse each other. "When they are in bed they sing and tell stories to each other and they then go to sleep." Sometimes these two help each other. A girl of 7 and her brother, aged 5, were often in a teacher-pupil relation. The mother of this boy and girl tells how this worked out.

> We have certain restrictions. We had to take the books out of the bookcase so the children wouldn't pull them out. Cynthia crawled and Charlie did not. But it was easier to train Charlie not to pull out the books because Cynthia would interest him in something else. Cynthia learned the alphabet from her blocks [and a baby sitter]. Later she sang the ABC song to Charlie. She has taught him to print and has tried to teach him to write, but I don't encourage that.

In another case the youngest of three girls does very advanced things for her age. The mother feels that the older girls are responsible for the rapid progress.

> Gail [aged 4] counts by 2's to 12 and by 10's to 100. She's been doing this for some time. It's funny to hear these things coming out of such a little thing. She picks them up from her older sisters. I didn't teach them to her.

Jealousy is thought to be the natural thing between siblings of close age if one receives some attention from the parents that the other does not. Parents try not to give one something without doing the same for the other.

A few extra years often tend to make an older sibling what parents consider to be "officious" toward his younger brothers and sisters. Such officious older siblings often act as the voice of conscience for all younger children in the family. Many older siblings are often very generous toward young brothers and sisters. Older children sometimes like to give the younger ones the benefits they feel they missed as children.

RELATIONSHIP TO FATHER

In the evening shortly before supper the father usually comes home. Three fathers in the sample traveled in their work and were home only a part of each week. Other fathers were occasionally away on business. On the other hand, seven sample fathers had jobs which allowed their children to accompany them at times during the week. These included tree work, selling eggs and produce house to house, painting, and construction.

The behavior of fathers toward their children is as varied as the time which they spend with them. Some fathers are enthusiastic about their work and spend little time at home and less still with their children. Others are felt to have a "tough row to hoe," and the mother may take as much responsibility around the home as she can to lighten their load. She may ask the children to leave the father in peace when he is at home. Still other fathers seek out their children and try to relieve the mother of duties, especially if there are a number of preschool children in the family.

Some fathers like to roughhouse with their children, and these especially enjoy preschool children. They would be afraid of treating a fragile infant in this way.

On weekends and in their brief vacations almost all fathers do odd jobs around their homes—repairs, mowing the lawn, or other heavy work in the yard. Most families own their homes, and the men seem to enjoy working around the house. The children, especially the boys, may tag along and help a little if the father is willing.

The father may also do some "baby-sitting" at times when he is home while the mother goes on errands or participates in womens' groups.

RELATIONSHIP TO ADULTS OUTSIDE THE FAMILY

Relations with adults outside the family are limited mostly to certain relatives and the mothers of playmates whom the preschool child visits. Each mother soon learns the standards which her neighbors set for their children, and most women conscientiously try to support each other in these matters. In emergencies neighbors occasionally help each other out with baby-sitting on a roughly reciprocal basis. However, it is expected that normally the mother herself will be responsible for her child and will be close enough so that she can hear him scream if he is in trouble.

GRANDMOTHERS

Many families have a grandmother or an aunt living nearby, who occasionally or frequently assumes the role of caretaker for the children. Some of these are almost complete mother substitutes, but others can be trusted with only the smallest child-care duties. Many grandparents, contrary to our expectations, are either ineffective or unwilling caretakers of their grandchildren. However, when a relative is involved in child-training, it is most usually the mother's mother. In six families in the sample, the mother's mother had occasional or frequent care of her grandchildren. Parents' sisters, brothers, and parents' aunts are sometimes reported as assisting in child care.

Grandmothers do not always love their grandchildren wholeheartedly. One grandmother was convinced that the observers represented substantiation of her own claim that the grandchild needed a psychiatrist. And some grandchildren do not like their grandparents.

My father's mother was a very funny person. I did not love her at all. She didn't let us call her Grandmother. We had to call her Nanna. She didn't want anybody to know she was a grandmother.

Pleasant relations with grandparents, however, are also frequent. One mother says, "All three of my children love my husband's mother to pieces. She is very good to them." One grandfather pleases his daughter-in-law: "But Grandpa doesn't think a child is good for much unless he works. It doesn't do children any harm to have the training like that [working with grandfather]."

If both parents and grandparents are present, discipline is generally left to the parents. Many mothers resent correction of their children by a grandparent. Others will allow it in the house of the grandparent. One grandparent, a mother's mother, who lived with the family, often "scolded" her grandchildren. The mother of the family said, "I think one person scolding a kid is enough, but sometimes we all get going and the kid gets off."

Although a grandmother often does not approve of the mother's discipline, she usually does not take disciplinary action herself. If grandparents have charge of a child, they generally try to distract the child rather than discipline him. Grandparents who want grandchildren to visit them report to the parent that the child "was wonderful."

BABY SITTERS

If a close relative is not available, all families will have a neighbor or a baby sitter who will take the mother's place on occasion. Some mothers only have a "sitter" in extreme emergencies; others will have one three or four hours each day. Baby sitters must be 12 years old to be left alone with a child, and preferably older. An unacceptable baby sitter is a girl who invites her male friends into the child's home while she is sitting. Mothers do not wish to be responsible for what may happen to a young girl under such circumstances. Some mothers will only have a baby sitter after the children are asleep, but this is not general.

In the new areas of town there are a number of groups of women who exchange baby sitting, especially daytime sitting, when a young child may be "parked" at a neighbor's house. Such a mother would be considered the most competent baby sitter.

There are a very few young male baby sitters in the town. These are all boys under 17 years of age, often relatives. Sometimes a kindly older woman will baby-sit for her younger women friends at no charge. Mothers generally would not call on such a woman except in an emergency, when no one else was available.

Baby sitters have varying authority. They are expected to see that the children behave but usually have no authority to punish. One mother, however, views this authority as necessary. "I tell the sitter she may, if she has to, spank. I know how kids can nag at you until you want just one swat." Another mother tells how her most frequent baby sitter "talks rough, but the children know how she means it."

While none of the preschool children in our sample were attending regular kindergarten during the course of our study, some did attend the Sunday School kindergarten or nursery while their parents went to church or their older brothers and sisters attended Sunday School proper. Little is demanded of preschool children in Sunday School. In the main, an effort is made to amuse them and keep them quiet so that they will not interfere with other activities. The main educational value of the Sunday School nursery and kindergarten is thought to be in accustoming the child to regular church attendance. When first left in the church nursery by their parents, many children cry loud and long. If it is warm weather and the windows are open, the crying can be heard plainly in the church, and the mother may have to return and quiet the child or remove him.

MOTHER'S ATTITUDE TOWARD
HER PARENTAL RESPONSIBILITIES

During the preschool period the mother continues to be the most important person in the child's life, although playmates, older siblings, and the father are of increasing importance. The mothers themselves accept the cultural doctrine of the importance of their child-care responsibilities, especially for younger children. Even when mother takes time off from these duties, she does so, ideally, for short periods when responsibilities are at a minimum. Thus many women report proudly that, "No one else has ever put my children to bed," or "No one else has ever had to feed my children." Mothers are supposed to supply love for their children. They are almost wholly responsible for their children's well-being—physical, mental, social.

Of course, none of the mothers studied conformed perfectly to their ideals of maternal behavior in actual practice. There are those who enjoy their responsibilities more than others and who make more elaborate and careful plans for their children. There are others who perform their duties with resignation. One woman reported that she "finally realized that I would have to give up my personal ambitions for the sake of the happiness of the whole family" and that she would have to accept this sacrifice more cheerfully. For the first few years she reported that she had found herself moody and discontented, clinging to her private ambitions.

Most mothers are able to express their own feelings toward the role they occupy. They say, "I often think I should never have been a mother" or "This is what I waited for all my life." Mothers often quite freely admit feelings of guilt in regard to responsibilities; they assign their failures to emotional or personal factors in themselves. They are constantly assessing their performances in terms of some ideal standard. The sanctions on the mother's behavior are important in this constant assessment. If mothers step beyond community standards, the force of gossip comes into play. A woman does not necessarily hear the gossip about herself, but she may imagine it from her private assessment of her own performance. It is not unusual for gossip to be repeated to her by a "friend." Whether or not a mother hears the stories told about her, she knows that no one is free from this sort of criticism, and she may hear others criticized for acts which she knows she has performed herself. From minor hints she may make conclusions which lead her to shift her behavior slightly. But the chief punisher of most deviating mothers is their own conscience.

If something happens to a mother, a substitute must be found immediately. Most people in the community cannot afford a paid mother substitute, and therefore a widower quickly remarries. There were no unmarried men with young children in the town. However, it is felt by most that no one is really able to substitute for the actual mother. Here is a statement by a woman who experienced a step-mother.

My true mother died when I was little and my stepmother was not very much of a success. I don't think stepmothers usually are, do you? I have called both my stepmothers by their first names. Definitely not "Mother"! I think you only have one mother. Not that I didn't like them. They were both all right, but they didn't take the place of my own mother.

MOTHER-CHILD INTERACTION

Analysis of behavioral observations collected during the study indicates that the mother's interaction with her preschool child is more generally involved with controlling the child by suggestions, command, or discipline than she is with helping. The behavioral observations also indicate that the more negative the mother is in dealing with the child—by negative we mean refusals of permission, criticism, etc.—the more negative the child is in response to the mother. There is also some indication that a mother is more likely to "push" a son in his activities than to push a daughter. In addition, the male children in the sample were much less verbal than the female children. Mothers are apt to try to draw out such a quiet son.

AUTHORITY OF THE FATHER

While the mother is in all families in charge of the preschool child more than the father by virtue of the fact that she is present more, in over half the families in our sample the father was said to exercise considerable authority over the child when he was present. Where this occurs it is a change from infancy, where the father, whatever his relations with his wife, has little to do with the child except occasional play and minor caretaking. In eight of the sample families the father tended to take the entire responsibility for discipline when he was around. On the other hand, in ten families the mother continued to do the disciplining even in the father's presence, while in the remainder the two parents shared authority.

When the authority is divided, the father will usually be the one to take final action. A mother who feels that she has been unsuccessful in getting her children to behave may invoke the father's name: "When Dad hears about this he's gonna be cross too," "I'll tell Dad when he gets home," "Do you want me to tell your Daddy?" "Your father will hear about this." Children are said to react differently. Some are afraid of father learning about bad behavior; others say, "Go ahead and tell him." In some families, as one woman says, "I would be wasting my breath saying 'wait until Daddy gets home,' because they know nothing's gonna happen when Daddy gets home."

Even when this technique is effective, mothers show some reluctance to invoke the father's name. It is generally felt that children should be punished on the spot as they misbehave, and it is an admission of failure for the mother to have to threaten the father's punishment. Moreover, some fathers seem to resent this disruption of their own relationship with the children, and some mothers are reluctant to call on their husbands for fear that they may punish the children too severely. One mother compared her own techniques of discipline to her husband's in describing the following incident:

> Tim broke a window at the neighbors. It was on a Thursday that he threw a stone and broke the window. The neighbor said to him, "Until you tell your mother you can't come back and play here." But Tim just stayed home and didn't tell us. Finally on Sunday the neighbor told us. I talked to my husband. Spanking wouldn't have done any good then; it was too long afterwards. My husband said we should take money from his allowance until it was paid for. But I said his punishment had been the scolding and not playing with the neighbor's boys. My husband would like to spank. Tim doesn't like to be spanked. . . . My husband has a heavy voice and it makes the children fear him. I say, you don't want them to fear you. We feared our father. . . . My husband is in favor of punishment. He thinks if they do something bad you should spank 'em or shake 'em to pieces. I don't see it that way.

The father's name is most often invoked in his absence when something in his precinct has been violated by the child, such as the use of his forbidden tools. One woman says that it is no use side-stepping most issues by mentioning father and so, "I use him on his hard and fast rules—just on the things he's strict on—he's a great one to say, 'Go ask your mother.' "

The relations between the parents are affected by the amount of discipline and care each is responsible for, and these relations in turn affect the children. The observers felt that almost all women with husbands who refused or participated grudgingly in child care and training had some resentment toward their husbands. This may be largely displaced onto the child, who is felt to be too much of a burden. The mildest cases of resentment are expressed by the women as "understanding" father's refusal to participate while still not liking it. More extreme cases of resentment often result in much bitterness.

Whatever the distribution between parents of authority over children, most parents agree that it is important to conceal disagreements from the children and present a united front. However, in at least half of the families indications were noted of some overt disagreement between parents as to standards of children's behavior. This seems to be especially characteristic of the early years of marriage.

RESPECT TO ADULTS

It is during the preschool period when most parents attempt to start instilling respect for adults. Tantrums, immoderate crying, or any open aggression against a parent, verbal or physical, all meet with parent's opposition.

Tantrums occur occasionally in preschool children, although in full-blown form they are rare or nonexistent in most school-age children. The common belief that they appear more frequently with a child whose mother indulges demands made in tantrums seems to be well justified. At an early age the mother may laugh tolerantly at the child's tantrums, but as school age approaches, more severe punishments are used. A teacher in a kindergarten to which a few North Village children had gone said:

Once in a while one has a tantrum, and you would have to pick them up bodily [and remove them from the room]. There should be no raising of the voice [of the teacher] except to make oneself heard. [Laughs]. [Mothers of children of this age would be less restrained.]

More common than full temper tantrums among children of this age is a tendency toward fussy crying when frustrated in some desire by a parent. All parents find this annoying at some point and come to feel somewhat like the mother who said: "That gets my goat; I mean fussy crying, not if he's really hurt. I get cross myself." Crying can be ignored by some parents, and is, when it is "attention crying," but more mothers are impelled to take some action.

She used to scream when I tried to correct her. So I'd take her into our great big bathroom and say, "Well, if you're gonna cry, you can cry in there where I can't hear you." . . . I never could stand a kid screaming when you corrected it. . . . I'll say, "Now you're not gonna start being a cry baby now, are you?" and if she's crying to get her own way, I'll say, "If you cry, I'll spank you." I never have, I don't have to.

Other parents in the same situation feel that crying is a necessity, but nevertheless annoying to the parent, and will tell the child, "Put your hand over your mouth" or "If you must cry, will you please cry in a quieter tone of voice." However, sensitivity is more allowable in girls than boys. Parents apparently sympathize with girls who have hurt feelings but try to get boys to be "brave little fellows."

DIRECT AGGRESSION AGAINST PARENTS

Preschool children at times react to parental frustration by direct aggression against the parents. Any serious attempts at physical aggression are usually punished by spanking or isolation. However, angry remarks by the child may be punished by sarcastic retorts or, occasionally, ignored if not too prolonged and repetitive, or if the child is known to be upset about something. Some parents try at times to eliminate the causes of anger or distract from the conflict situation. About half of the mothers say they want their children to be able to admit it when they are irritated and angry but to control the feeling to the extent that they can reach a reasonable solution to the problem.

Even joking or play aggression toward the parents usually meets with some retaliation. Parents fear joking may get out of hand if not controlled. A little more aggression is allowed toward parents in public because parents are embarrassed to punish a child publicly. One 4-year-old boy sometimes called his mother an "old witch." This was considered to be a family joke, and it is unknown whether the mother punished this in private. One boy showed a lot of fantasy aggression toward his mother. He had many plans to scare her and so on. This was considered funny. One child sometimes speaks of "those lousy parents." Other people are amused by this although they might disapprove of it in their own child.

AGGRESSION TOWARD PEERS

A child's expression of anger toward his peers is much less subject to parental reprimand than anger toward the parents, especially for boys. Arguing and mild physical fighting may even be encouraged by parents as defensive measures if they feel that another child is dominating or bullying their own child. This is especially common with fathers and sons. There are definite parental limits on children's aggression toward peers, however. Children should not use profane or obscene words and must be careful in their fighting not to cause serious permanent injury to the other child. Throwing rocks or using sticks and clubs is generally taboo and severely punished if discovered. Very little attempt is made to control playful aggression of children toward peers as long as it does not degenerate into bullying or result in too much "excitement." In one observation a child busily prepared "poison" clay cookies for a small guest expected in the afternoon. This was considered to be funny. Parents themselves would not participate in such fantasies if asked by their children, and generally pretend not to see or hear them, but they do not overtly censure the child for them.

PARENTAL ATTITUDE TOWARD HAPPINESS

Parents, especially mothers, are concerned that their children should give evidence of happiness and positive emotion. If the child has been to a neighbor's house, the standard questions on return include "Did you have a good time?" If a child appears to be sad about something, or perhaps merely thoughtful, the parent is likely to ask, "What's the matter with you?" and advise the child to smile. If they have time, they may play with him a little to make him feel better.

On the other hand, excessively boisterous good spirits are also frowned on. Parents usually reprimand loud shouting by children, especially if by girls and in the house.

Children anticipating special events often get quite excited, too much so according to some parents. Some were even said to get so excited that they did not enjoy the events themselves. One or two families solve this by not telling the child about the event in advance. Almost all parents take the precaution of not telling children about a prospective event unless it is certain to take place. They feel that the pain of disappointment is too great for children to bear and recall their own disappointments in childhood. One mother said that she was "tempted to paddle" when the child gets "all worked up" but that she restrains herself. Evidently too much excitement is regarded as exhausting and threatening to discipline and scheduling.

The desire to have the child give evidence of happiness is connected with the parents' desire to prove to themselves that they have done their duty and that the child is accordingly developing properly. A related manifestation is a certain amount of encouragement to the child for "showing off" his accomplishments to the parents and interested visitors. Showing off is encouraged more in early childhood than at any other period in the child's life, and most children develop the propensity sufficiently that by the time they enter school controls must be imposed by both parents and teachers. In the preschool period, however, controls on excessively prolonged showing off are relatively mild. The parents may simply cease paying attention to the child, put on a disgusted face, or suggest to him that he is making a fool of himself.

A certain amount of showing off in early childhood is considered desirable in order to overcome the child's shyness of people outside the family, although the term itself, a "show-off" is derogatory. Parents do not want their children to be unnecessarily afraid of anyone or of anything, and showing off develops social courage in the child and may encourage specific learning.

The intentional cultivation of irrational fears of strange people or places as a device for keeping children out of places they should not be is recognized as a possible effective technique but is considered to be lazy and unscrupulous on the part of the adult and damaging to the child's confidence in the world. One mother criticized a relative, saying:

Aunt May used to say to her "Oh don't go in there, it's dark!" . . . You could tell them they might stumble over things without any light on, that they should be careful, but I don't see scaring them that way. She also picked up a fear of mice from May. Even now she has a lot of fears and is scared to go upstairs.

SUMMARY

To summarize the major developments in early childhood (preschool), the child becomes more sociable and develops significant relationships with persons outside his household, especially with the small neighborhood play group, but also with adult neighbors and relatives. Along with this the child acquires fairly good control of overt intense aggression. He can meet an increasing number of needs by himself. Differentiation between boys and girls starts to be important in this period: boys are supposed to be physically aggressive in self-defense while girls are supposed to defend themselves only verbally; boys' pastimes are supposed to be more athletic, while girls are supposed to be more interested in imitating or trying to help their mother.

Chapter 16

First and Second Grades

When a child reaches the age of 6, or just before his sixth birthday, his life changes; he is now eligible for first grade and required by law to attend school. For six hours a day he is away from home with a new adult in charge, a teacher rather than his mother, and a large group of same-aged peers. Most of the time he is confined to one room and is required to sit in a chair for long periods of time, leaving the room only with the permission of the teacher. He must wait his turn to speak and do what is required of him by the teacher and schedule. He is ready to begin his formal training in certain basic skills highly valued by American culture and to receive training in differential sex-role behavior. Schedules and clocks become important pressures in his life.

MORNING ROUTINE

On school days children now have to be prompt about getting up in the morning, for they must be at school on time. One boy, aged 7, is said, during the school year, to wake up at 7:00 along with his parents and have breakfast. He usually dresses, after finishing his breakfast, in time to catch the school bus at 7:55, arriving at school at 8:25.

Another mother reports that her daughter of the same age arises at 6:30. The alarm goes off in the parents' room at 6:45. From 6:45 to 7:30 the children play in their bedroom, playing on their beds often. Breakfast is ready at 7:30; it takes about ten minutes. The girl dresses herself, gets on the school bus at 8:00, and gets to school about 8:25. It is clear that there is not much time for interaction with either parent before leaving for school.

If possible, children of school age are more likely to have bedrooms of their own than preschool children, but, again, most of the children in the sample with siblings of the same sex were sleeping in the same room with them. One mother expressed concern that her daughter, aged 7, still had to sleep in a room with her son, aged 5, because the father had not yet finished off additional sleeping space upstairs in their house.

Children do not generally wash themselves extensively in the morning because they have often had a bath the previous evening and gone to bed clean. However, they may brush their teeth before going off to school.

Most children of school age dress themselves. Mothers feel that it is inappropriate to help them and report feeling guilty if they do. The mother feels she may legitimately help comb hair, or braid it in the case of a girl, and she may button back buttons. A few children in the sample were reported to receive "more help than they should." It is felt that boys of this age are apt to "dawdle" in getting dressed or undressed, a source of irritation to the mother.

Even when children dress themselves, the mother may still lay out the child's clothes for him, although some mothers even allow the children of early school age to pick out their clothes for the day by themselves. One mother felt that her daughter would best learn how to choose suitable combinations of clothes to wear by being given freedom at this age and allowed to experience criticism for poor choices. However, in any case, at this age children are generally not allowed to choose which clothes the mother will buy for them, although she may take into account their preferences.

Some have special "school clothes" for their children, which are worn only in school or when going someplace out of the neighborhood. After school these children then change into "play clothes," with which they may be more careless. Other parents may dress their children as well, but do not have such a marked division between school and play clothes.

Before girls reach school age they sometimes wear trousers to play in, especially in cold weather. However, once they reach school age, they regularly wear skirts, differentiating them clearly in dress from the boys. This sex distinction in dress is one sign suggesting that the early grades of school are regarded as the time when children learn most about public sex roles. Children are not expected to learn about the "facts of life" at this time, but it is thought that they come to recognize the general psychological and behavioral differences between the sexes and learn the appropriate type of behavior for their own sex.

Once a child starts school, eating a good breakfast becomes more important. A typical breakfast for one child consisted of orange juice, cocoa, egg, or cereal. The "energy" from breakfast is supposed to last the child through the morning at school. With a preschooler this is less of a problem, for the mother may allow a snack or arrange an early lunch if she feels the child needs it. One mother said she believed that her children were not doing as well as they might in school because they were eating poorly.

THE SCHOOL BUS

At the time of our study nearly all first and second grade children went to school by bus, since the school was located in a sparsely settled area intermediate between the three centers of population of the town. The bus stopped at definite places on a fixed schedule. The schedule and route were changed each year, however, so that no one part of town is always the earliest.

Most North Village parents felt that the elementary school was within possible but not easy walking distance for their children, and that by this age the children could, if necessary, manage the traffic on the local roads. Most parents tried to avoid giving their children the idea that it was safe to miss the bus. One mother said, "Don't come back home if you miss the bus; just start walking." This mother was chagrined to find that her dawdling daughter had not learned her lesson from this, for a friendly neighbor had picked her up on the street and driven her to school. However, some mothers would "break down" and take a late child to school in the family car, perhaps ostensibly on the ground that walking would be too slow.

The children's behavior on the bus is a problem at times for the driver, who is supposed to keep order at the same time that he drives. One threat which he can invoke is to put unruly children off the bus and make them walk. There were no instances of children being put off the bus on the way to school, but there were a few instances of this happening on the way home. One mother was very angry when her son was disciplined by being put off the bus. She felt it was the bus driver's responsibility to bring him home or to notify her that he was walking.

SCHOOL SCHEDULE

On arrival at school the children go immediately to their rooms, take off their coats, and go to their seats to wait for the opening exercises. The teacher often uses this time before formal opening to talk informally with the class as a group. The children may also read to themselves or color in their workbooks individually at this time. Quiet talking is allowed.

Opening exercises vary somewhat according to the teacher's preferences but generally include a recital of the Lord's Prayer (Protestant version) and the pledge of allegiance to the flag by the children, all standing, the reading of a Bible passage by the teacher (especially one of the more popular psalms), and the singing of a hymn or "My Country 'Tis of Thee." The children recite the prayer and pledge rapidly in wooden fashion, although the teachers themselves read and recite expressively. These exercises are legally required, and while there appears to be little interest in them, there is also little opposition to them. The elementary school principal said that one child, whose parents were Jehovah's Witnesses, had been excused from the recitation of the pledge of allegiance with little question.

Each teacher prepares her own schedule for covering the required material in the curriculum and submits this to the principal for approval periodically. The actual order of subjects for any one day in a class depends partly on the teacher's preferences and partly on whether there are any special subjects which interrupt the regular routine. The special subjects include physical education, music, and art. Each class receives a half-hour visit every other week from a special instructor in these subjects who works with all the classes in the Orchard Town school system. However, the regular teachers are supposed to allow some additional class time apart from the special periods for art and music, and this they generally do.

The teachers tend to have the subjects demanding the most attention at the beginning of the school day but also tend to intersperse periods of concentrated attention with simpler activities. Reading or arithmetic is a common first subject, while penmanship, drawing, spelling, and so on, would tend to come later.

READING

For reading, but not other subjects, the elementary children are divided into three groups on the basis of ability. The teacher works with each group in turn at a special table in the front of the room, while the rest of the children are at their seats busy with their workbooks or, if these are finished, drawing, reading, or playing with small educational games or puzzles.

The general pattern of teaching is for the teacher to alternate between explaining things to the class and calling on the children to
answer questions or read certain passages. When she is dealing with
the whole class, she may ask the children to volunteer to answer by
raising their hands to avoid the confusion of several simultaneous answers or she may again ask a specific child to answer or recite. In the
small reading groups, the children generally read in turn, going
around the table, and answer questions freely and informally. Most
children are eager to "show off" their knowledge, especially when they
perceive another child is in difficulty, and when the teacher has asked
one child to recite, she often has some trouble restraining the other
children from volunteering an answer.

At 10 o'clock the first grade has fifteen minutes of recess, which is
immediately followed by a period of the same length for the second
grade. Before going out to recess, the teachers remind the children to
go to the "basement" if they need to. "Basement" is a euphemism for
toilet. In the new all-town elementary school everything is on one floor,
but in the old separate village schools the toilet was in the basement.

RECESS

Recess is rather disorganized. The children spend most of their time
running around chasing each other. Boys and girls generally stay on
separate sides of the building. The sexes do mix a little near the end
of the building, and the teachers do little to prevent this, but in general the children themselves seem to desire the separation and maintain it.

The principal had tried to arrange organized games for the first and
second graders during recess and said she had had no trouble doing
this in earlier times when the older classes were in the same school and
the young children could follow the model of the older grades whom
they saw playing games. However, the attempt to organize games for
the large number of elementary children without this model had in
the main failed. Perhaps the greater number of children of the same
age all together on one playground also hindered organization of
games. It may also be that organized games would work with more
adult supervision. At any one recess two of the four first or second
grade teachers are out on the playground, one for the boys and
one for the girls, while the other two are free to remain inside and
prepare materials.

The children are taught organized games in the special weekly gym period and play them with interest at this time. The teacher-pupil ratio here is more favorable, since only one room has gym at a time. Also, boys and girls are mixed in the gym period, which seems to calm down the boys somewhat.

The children always go outside at recess unless it is snowing hard or raining. On very cold, windy, winter days the recess period may be shortened a little by teachers, however, and if the playground is covered with deep snow, the children may simply march in a line around the cleared roads and paths.

There is some difference between boys' and girls' activities in recess. Jumping rope is popular mainly with girls. Both sexes play with balls. The boys form "gangs" under the leadership of a physically powerful (and often intellectually backward) boy and go charging about the playground playfully scaring nonmembers. Serious fights do not generally issue from these gang activities, perhaps partly because the teachers try to keep them somewhat under control. Many boys of this age, whether members of a gang or not, regard the gangs as very important.

Once in a while two boys will get into a fight on the playground. One fight which was observed involved an argument over a place in line as the children line up to go back in their rooms. A teacher stopped it promptly and scolded the fighters severely. Teachers are generally less sympathetic than parents to claims of self-defense.

LUNCH

Lunch for both grades takes place at 11:30 in order to clear the lunchroom for the junior high and high school children who also use the same room. The first grade goes in about five minutes ahead of the second, which follows when they can be served. Teachers see that the children all wash their hands before going to lunch.

Most children take advantage of the hot lunch served by the school at a nominal cost, although parents are free to have the children carry their lunch to school, and a few children do this. These children do not go through the full cafeteria line and eat together at a separate table. Some children also eat a candy bar or other snack at recess, and one teacher often gave her children crackers at this time.

The school authorities and some of the parents expressed the belief that the school lunch program is educational as well as simply supplying needed food. They believe that the school lunches help the children learn to eat a variety of foods and a well-balanced diet. Since the school receives federal aid for lunches, the menus must meet certain specifications as to quantity and types of food. The weekly menu at the school cafeteria is published in the local paper and duplicated to be taken home to parents so that the mother can avoid preparing the same food at home on the same day and ensure a variety of food for the child.

At school some of the teachers put a little pressure on children to eat, although probably considerably less than at home on the average. For example, the teacher may ask a girl, "Did you finish your milk?" In the cafeteria there is a rule that children may not have seconds until they have eaten everything on their tray. Parents generally seem to approve of this, although some think it amusing that a child had to finish his dessert before getting a second helping of a main course.

After lunch, for which twenty minutes are allowed, there is another recess period and free period. Possibly the point of this is to duplicate the longer lunch periods of the older grades, where some children go home for lunch. The second grade is out for twenty minutes starting at 11:50, and the first grade is out for a similar period starting at 12:10 after spending the preceding twenty minutes in leisure activities in their rooms. Activities in the noon recess are similar to the earlier morning recess.

CLASSES AFTER LUNCH

After the noon recess there is still some class time left. This is a time for activities regarded by the children as more "fun"—drawing or music, spelling or arithmetic "bees" where the class may be divided up into teams which compete in answering the teacher's questions, and so forth. In conclusion, the teacher often reads a story to the children, to which most of them listen attentively.

At the end of the school day the children reassemble in bus groups, that is, the children going to the various villages, who are scattered among the four classrooms in each grade, assemble in a single room, most often not their own. This a time of some tension, for the children are supposed to be orderly but are liable to get into arguments about places in line or whether they have on their outdoor clothes properly. Some of the teachers at this time appear to be more critical of children from other rooms than of their own children. The feeling was occasionally expressed by some that their colleagues handled these children less competently than they would. The teacher's attitude toward children from another room appears to be much like a parent's attitude toward children from another family and is indicative of the sort of personal attachment which teachers in the early grades develop toward their pupils.

RELATIONSHIP TO TEACHER

While most of the first and second grade teachers might be regarded as "motherly" individuals, there are important differences in the relationships of mothers and teachers to their children. On the one hand, the teacher has a less intense relationship to her pupils than the mother. She has close contact with them for only one year and also has nearly 30 small children at a time as opposed to one or a few which a mother might have. But, on the other hand, the teacher demands much more of the child than the mother does, at least at this age. She requires him to spend much time in "school work"—which he may not always want to do—and prevents him from doing a number of other things which would interfere with his own work or, worse yet, the work of other members of his class.

The child soon learns that he may not talk as freely as at home. He may not talk out loud when the teacher is talking and when other children are reciting. Elementary teachers do not invariably require their pupils to raise their hands whenever they want to say something to the class, but when several children wish to talk at once, the teacher invokes the hand-raising rule to preserve order. The teacher likes to encourage each child to contribute to class discussion and recitation. This means that the children must "take turns" in talking and that opportunities to "show off" are limited. Moreover, while the teachers try to avoid open criticism of a child who is doing his best, however poor that may be, their praise of a child's remarks or recitation is not so lavish or indiscriminate as many parents'. The children themselves are jealous of each other for receiving the teacher's attention or praise, and criticism which the teacher herself leaves unsaid may be uttered by the other children.

The teacher imposes restrictions on the children's physical movement as well as on their talking. During recitation periods the children involved are supposed to sit quietly in their seats, and even in periods when the child is supposed to be working by himself, the teacher may require him to obtain permission before leaving his seat to go to the toilet, sharpen a pencil, and so on.

Both parents and teachers recognize that it is hard for children to keep still in school. The first grade teachers especially seemed tolerant of minor infractions. When nothing is happening to which the children should be attending, they are allowed to talk quietly or whisper to each other. At other times whispering, if noticed at all, often brings reproof or reminder. Talking over work assignments with other pupils is discouraged officially, although one visiting mother expressed surprise at how much one teacher permitted children to help each other.

TEACHING TECHNIQUES

In addition to the various restrictions on the children's activity, the teacher makes many positive demands with regard to school work. The child is asked to finish various lessons within a specified time, and he is asked to do them with a reasonable degree of understanding. If his attention wanders and he fails to do his work through apparent lack of serious intent, the teacher may mention his failure before the class. If he does the required work well, he will very probably be praised strongly before the class, and the teacher may show his paper or other work to the class as a model.

Skillfully allotted verbal praise and, to a lesser extent, fairly mild ridicule are the main disciplinary techniques now used by Orchard Town teachers from the elementary grades on. Some corporal punishment was used in the school days of the parents of the present children, but this has now practically vanished. However, some instances which some people interpreted as corporal punishment continue to occur occasionally. One teacher, for instance, was vaguely alleged to have knocked two boys' heads together "or maybe hit them on the head with a book." One teacher described another teacher shaking a child but felt this had little effect on the child. A few young children reported corporal punishment. These reports often seem exaggerated.

In extreme cases of disorder or disobedience a child may be moved to a corner of the room or sent to the hall for a while or to see the principal. The principal may simply repeat the scolding already administered by the teacher or may notify the child's mother.

Making a child stay after school is not used as a punishment in the first two grades, probably because this would make the child miss his bus, and the teacher could not easily assume the responsibility for getting him home.

Verbal praise is sometimes supplemented, in the early grades especially, with charts listing the members of the class on which the teacher pastes stars by the children's names as tokens of recognition for their good behavior, neatness, or other nonscholastic virtues. One second grade teacher allowed the children to choose who would get a star and who should not and pointed out to them, "Your own peers are choosing." Evidently one of the purposes of this was to eliminate a feeling on the part of the children who did not receive stars that they were being treated unfairly by the teacher.

Another form of positive reward which the teachers use is in the assignment of minor tasks about the classroom, such as passing out and collecting papers, erasing the blackboard, or running small errands for the teacher. Children regard being assigned such tasks as a sign that the teacher trusts them and thinks well of them, and the teachers use the assignment of tasks quite explicitly to reward children who are well behaved or have done well scholastically. No instances were observed of a teacher asking for volunteers in assigning some job or some minor errand and not getting a response from the class. As a rule, not everyone responds, but each time there are practically always a number of children from whom the teacher may select one. Probably, however, children who volunteer too frequently or who are chosen by the teacher too frequently would be derided as "teacher's pet."

EMOTIONAL DISTURBANCES

The sudden change from home to school, with its greater demands, produces signs of emotional disturbance in some of the children. A few children, for instance, start to wet their pants in school, apparently after having learned to control themselves adequately at home. It is perhaps significant that one first grade teacher who was especially patient and fairly permissive reported that she had never had children with this problem. Teachers are on the alert for this kind of thing and urge children, on occasion, to go to the toilet. The children feel, rightly or wrongly, that they have to ask permission to leave the room to go to the toilet. This is not supposed to be so in some rooms in the first two grades, and perhaps children confuse this with the need to ask permission to get a drink of water. At lunch time, even in the third to sixth grades, teachers were heard to remind children to go to the toilet.

Some children show other signs of emotional disturbance about the demands of school. One girl was frequently absent because of illnesses which her mother admitted were at least in part feigned. But this mother said proudly, "Even with all her absences she can keep up with the others." One boy, who is thought of by his parents and teachers to be a "genius," is said to cry when he does not get the highest mark in his class. Another cried when his cat did not win a prize in a school pet show.

ATTEMPTS TO MAKE SCHOOL ENJOYABLE

Perhaps in part to compensate for these demands on the children, elementary teachers make a conscious effort to make school enjoyable for their pupils. Attempts are made with humor to entice the children to study. An elementary arithmetic workbook, for instance, was entitled "Jolly Numbers." Or, again, for writing practice a humorous poem may be given, as the following:

> Is a caterpillar ticklish?
> Well it is always my belief
> That he giggles as he wiggles
> Across a hairy leaf.

Apart from this attempt to rouse interest in what is thought of as basically "work," there is also the introduction of certain activities which the children think of primarily as "fun." These would include singing favorite songs, telling the teacher and class about interesting experiences out of school, drawing and coloring, playing with puzzles, and so on, for children who have finished other work.

Of course, Orchard Town teachers are not unique in their attempt to make school enjoyable for young children; they simply exemplify a national trend in this respect. In fact, the system does not claim to keep up with the latest educational fashions and has never reached the extremes of indulgence of pupils attained by some other schools at the height of the progressive movement.

This concern with making schools enjoyable is not limited to professional teachers but is widespread among the parents of the community. The new elementary school building and other new buildings planned at the time of our study also reflect the same general attitude on the part of the community. Most people regarded it as axiomatic that the new buildings should be more comfortable and attractive to the children than the old schools.

Teachers evidently sense the concern of the majority of parents that their children should enjoy school. There seemed to be an assumption that if a parent or other adult came to visit a class, he or she would want to see, most of all, evidence that the children were having a good time. Thus one teacher, whose classroom one of us visited for the first time, interrupted her regular class work to show how one of her brighter pupils could organize a play around a Russian folk tale, choosing some of the other children in the class as actors. Another teacher commented about her class during a sort of recreational period, which may well have been arranged or prolonged for the observer's benefit, saying "See how relaxed they are; I think it is wonderful!"

Attempts to interest the children in school by such indulgence reduce the time available for conventional study. Whether for this reason or because of the general hurried pace of American life, some of the teachers repeatedly expressed the feeling, "There is not enough time."

It is hard to know how much effect the teacher's efforts to make school attractive have, but most of the children seem to come to accept school as largely pleasant or at least not highly unpleasant. Truancy is not a serious problem now in Orchard Town. The parents want their children to attend school, and there are not too many attractions outside the school to entice the children to "play hookey."

PARENT TEACHER RELATIONSHIP

Although control of the child at this age for much of the weekday is relinquished by the parents to the teacher, the parents' continuing concern for their child is manifested in part by an interest in what the teacher is doing. Parents tend to be most active in the Parent-Teacher Association when they have a child in the early grades. Some mothers visit their children's classes in grade school to see how they are making out and to become acquainted with the teacher. The institution of a "room mother" flourished in the first two grades. This is a mother of one of the children who helps the teacher arrange special celebrations of holidays.

Parents are always concerned about reports that the teacher has disciplined their child, although their reaction varies from resentment to approval. The opposition of these two agents of discipline is not as strong as it might be, though, since the children do not report most of their punishments to their parents. We were more likely to hear about these than the parents. If parents are particularly upset by some action on the part of the teacher, the mother often "goes down to school to have it out" with her. In these instances they generally tend to feel that the teacher is just as much at fault as the child, even after they hear the teacher's side of the story. Some parents try to side with the teacher, feeling that the child is the sufferer when the disciplinarians are at odds or even that the teacher is probably right. Often, however, parents feel teachers misunderstand their children and therefore are bad teachers, while teachers feel parents have "spoiled" the children in some respect.

COMPARING CHILDREN

Both parents and teachers keep track of the childrens' work, compare the work of various children with each other, and on occasion call their findings to the attention of the children—as a reward to successful children and as a standard of achievement for the less successful. One parent reported that when she went to school, her teacher used to tell her, "All your brothers and sisters got A's; why can't you?"

Currently both parents and teachers have some tendency to be careful about openly comparing children with each other on the subject of academic achievement because of the belief that children will be "hurt" if they are not able to meet the standards set by other children. However, because of numerous parental remarks in the preschool period, the children come to school with a keen sensitivity as to how they stand in comparison with other children of their age, and it is not difficult for them to infer their approximate relative scholastic standing even if the teacher refrains from open direct comparison. For one thing, papers are often graded on a numerical point system and, if not, then with letters. Children can and do compare these. While the teachers do not always single out the least successful student for ridicule, they often, perhaps, achieve a similar effect by singling out the best student for special praise.

We have previously noted the division of the class into three reading groups according to individual ability. These are most important in first and second grades, for learning to read takes up more of the school day there than in the higher grades. In fact, by fifth grade this division is dropped. Everyone, including the children, knows which reading group is the best one, the worst, and the intermediate, although the teachers go out of their way to avoid mentioning this as a rule. Some teachers refer to the reading groups by the book they may be reading at the time. One teacher numbered the groups but reversed the order of the numbering, that is, the "first" reading group was actually the lowest in ability. In the first and second grades some give the reading groups names, such as Busy Bees, Butterflies, Bluebirds, and Pigeons.

Both parents and teachers at times make invidious comparisons without fully realizing what they are doing. In the following example the teacher intended to encourage the child by publicly noting improvement in her work, but one may wonder if this was actually the main effect.

Well, Susan, you ought to be complimented. Look at the difference from the work she did yesterday. [Teacher holds up Susan's book and shows the class. She then shows the class Susan's work of yesterday.] Do any of you like the work she did yesterday?
Several children: Awful! Awful!
Don't you like to do good work, Susan?
Susan [softly, as if embarrassed]: Yes.

AFTER SCHOOL PLAY

As soon as children get off the school bus, they generally go home promptly and report to their mothers before they do anything else. On the way back from school they may have arranged to play with other schoolmates after checking in at home. The mothers generally approve of these plans, but if a child succumbs to the temptation to go directly to a friend's house without reporting first, he is severely punished. The punishment would be especially severe if the friend lived in another part of the village and the child were not in the habit of visiting there.

When the children get home, many mothers are in the habit of giving them a cookie, glass of milk, or other snack. Perhaps the mothers feel that the children have not been given as much food as they need in school. Some of these same mothers also give their children a little food to take to school in the morning for a snack at recess time.

If the weather is at all suitable, the children usually go outside to play with friends immediately after their snack or, in some families, after changing into play clothes.

PLAYMATES

Playmates are generally chosen from the other children of the same sex in the neighborhood. However, the range of houses which the elementary school child may visit freely is somewhat larger than preschool child's range, and by special arrangements he may at times visit school friends who live in other parts of town. Play groups of children of this age at home, as at school recess, are usually segregated by sex. However, the age segregation found at school is not found at home. We regularly observed children of this age playing with children as much as three or four years older or younger. The population of Orchard Town is dispersed enough so that a strict age segregation would leave many children without any nearby playmates of the same sex.

Perhaps one important reason for the segregation of sexes in play at this age is that by now physical aggression, both playful and serious, has practically ceased in girls while it continues to be important in boys. The elementary school girls at any rate say that they want to play by themselves because the boys are too "rough."

Play groups of grade school children after school are usually small, although a child may have a fairly large number of children with whom he plays during the year. For one thing, the mothers discourage large play groups by not allowing them access to the house. But apart from this there is no very clear authority structure in the play groups, and in groups of more than two or three children there is trouble in deciding what the group is to do. In a group of two or three, the children are held together by a need for companionship, and the compromise of differences is fairly simple, but larger groups can, and easily do, break into smaller groups without leaving any child without a playmate.

Although it is true that the play groups have no formal authority, first and second grade children are keenly aware of relative status, and certain children are more admired than others. This status is based much more on individual achievement and personality traits than on the socio-economic status in the community of adult members of the family. When children of this age meet for the first time, therefore, they are concerned with establishing their relative achievements. We give below an example of this kind of behavior in a conversation which took place between a 6-year-old girl visiting our house for the first time and our elder daughter (then aged 4).

Daughter: I can climb a ladder. [There is a ladder resting on a fence.]
Girl: *I* can climb a ladder—*that* ladder.
Daughter: I can climb *any* ladder.
Girl: So can I. Can you dance?
Daughter: No.
Girl: *I* can dance.
Daughter: I can dance around in a circle.
Girl: Oh, I can do *that*. I can *really* dance—ballet dance.
Daughter: I can do Farmer-in-the-Dell.
Girl: Oh anybody can do *that*. . . . I had my nursery school at home and my mother was the teacher and another lady. . . . I can go on a trapeze.
Daughter: I can sit on a trapeze.
Girl: Oh, that's easy. I'll tell you what I can do: I can *write*. Can you?
Daughter: No.

Girl: I can read, too. Can you read?
Daughter: No.
Girl: Can you keep quiet? (Laughing) *I* can.
Daughter: I *don't.*
Girl: . . . the teacher wants you to keep quiet. She says "keep quiet, shut up."
    (But some children) . . . even talk louder when she says that. . . . I got
    three teeth out. Have you got any out?
Daughter: I haven't even got a rotten tooth.
Girl: *I* don't have any rotten teeth. When you get two teeth out you get
    twenty cents and when you get one tooth out you get ten cents. (Laughs)

There is no sudden change in play activity around home once the
children enter school. However, organized outdoor games, such as tag,
hide-and-seek, varieties of baseball (for the boys) which require only
a few players, and so on, become of some importance. The children
learn some of these games in gym periods at school but more of them
from older playmates around the neighborhood whom they have observed playing such games although they were excluded from them.

There are also a number of relatively unorganized recreational activities or games played, but even here there are often many rules and
restrictions of the activities. For instance, "Cowboys" appears to be
a rather formless game, if it can even be called a game, but still it has
certain rules: sides must be chosen, and the children at least try to
come to some agreement as to when someone is properly "shot dead."
Children of the ages which we studied all occasionally play "Cowboys,"
although children over the age of 6 played this more often, and boys
played more than girls. Two adult informants said that they believed
that children played "Cowboys" much more now than they used to
because of watching Westerns on television. One wonders if it is not a
modern version of "cops-and-robbers."

"Cowboys" is usually played outside, although a large barn or large
basement or a place large enough for hiding and making surprise "at-
tacks" is a possible setting. An ordinary playroom or bedroom is not
satisfactory for this. An area of several adjoining yards is ideal. Children make limits or bounds within which the players are supposed to
stay.

SUPERVISION OF PLAY AND CONTROL OF AGGRESSION

There is somewhat less adult supervision of the school age children's
play than of the preschool children's play. People feel that their children need to learn how to get along with others in these groups and

that adult interference or protection may prevent the child from learn-ing this important lesson. Adult intervention is generally regarded as undesirable "as long as nobody is getting hurt."

Parents will not only control their own impulses to intervene and settle quarrels of their children with their playmates but will also often refuse to intervene even when requested by the child. Both mothers and fathers, but especially fathers, may encourage a son to fight against another boy of equal size and age in retaliation. Girls are not encouraged to fight physically but are encouraged to stand up for their rights in verbal argument.

There are definite limits on the sort of physical fighting permitted for boys, however. Kicking, throwing rocks, and hitting with objects other than one's hands are forbidden. During our year of observation one boy hit another on the head with a milk bottle. The offending boy was punished by making him stay at home in his own yard. Siblings of the injured boy went about the neighborhood hinting that doctor bills would be sent to the parents of the offending boy. No doctor was actually called in the case, however.

Very little physical fighting, either play or serious, was observed among girls of elementary school age or older. They fought neither with boys nor with each other. Some exceptions were occasional snow-ball fights in the winters, the playful roughhousing of three sisters, carefully supervised by the mother, and the playful chasing of some 10-year-old girls. All of these were less violent than similar activity of boys of the same ages.

Roughhousing between boys is permitted in the yard but usually causes some anxiety. A parent may warn, "You better stop or some-body's gonna get hurt." When the weather permitted, groups of young boys would gather on our back lawn to "wrestle." Occasionally such play battles ended on a sour note and someone would go angrily home. Snowballing is also permitted within the same bounds as roughhous-ing. If someone gets hurt or angry, the game breaks up.

On the rare occasions when a parent intervenes, he will generally discipline a play group only by reprimanding his own children. Occa-sionally a parent may rebuke a neighbor's child, but this is probably an impulsive act stemming from sudden anger and apt to be resented by the child's parents if they learn of it. One woman said of such an impulsive neighbor, "We are not speaking to each other. We found that we were being told what we could do even in our yard." On the other hand, as long as the neighbors exercise restraint in dealing with a couple's children, the parents try to make their children behave in a manner acceptable to the neighbors. As one mother said:

If the neighbors don't approve of something, I try to give the kids their side of it too. That's why I think the child has it so doggone hard, because they're called to account by so many people. If I don't teach them, they're going to learn it from somebody outside anyway.

PARENTAL CRITICISM OF PLAY

Although parents try to give the play groups considerable autonomy, they do continue to exercise some influence, mostly indirect, on their elementary school child's choice of playmates. Mothers sometimes make critical remarks to their child about undesired playmates and also show differential hospitality to neighbor's children according to their suitability as playmates from the point of view of morals and manners.

Another parental consideration affecting the composition of play groups is a feeling that each set of neighborhood parents should take its share of responsibility for supervision of the neighborhood children. One's own children, it is felt, should not spend too much time visiting the neighbors and "making trouble for them," and, reciprocally, the neighbors should not let their children spend too much time away from home. Thus, while absolute rules, such as "You must never go to the Doe's," are rare, a mother may very well say, "Don't go over to the Doe's today, you've been spending too much time over there," or she may be less hospitable to the Doe children if she thinks they have been spending too much time at her own house.

SOLITARY ACTIVITIES

There are a few solitary activities in which some children spend a considerable amount of their free time. Watching television is one of these, although often two or three children watch a program together. Also, as soon as they learn to read fairly well (often, by second grade), many children spend some time in the house reading children's books. There is a branch of the town library in North Village which has children's books and is open at certain hours. Parents who buy books for their children often give these to the town library when their children have outgrown or become tired of them. Such reading, of course, is unsupervised except that parents may encourage their children to take out books, probably in the hope of improving their reading ability.

Children who take piano lessons are required to spend a certain amount of time each day practicing. Piano lessons may be started at the elementary school level. Probably a minority of the children actually take piano lessons, since not all homes have pianos or the money to pay the teacher, and since there is a feeling that the child should want to take lessons before he is allowed to do so. Of the 24 families in our sample, at least 3 had children taking lessons. The piano teachers are mainly a few housewives who give lessons to earn extra income. As a rule, parents do not teach their own children.

SPECIAL ACTIVITIES

Activities on Saturdays and during school vacations are much like after-school activities except that there is more time for the mother to take the children on occasional special trips, such as to the movies, to ponds for swimming in warm weather, and so forth.

SUNDAY SCHOOL

Sundays bring a change for many elementary school children in that this is the age of greatest attendance at Sunday School. Starting with children of this age, the Sunday School proceedings are divided into two parts: a worship service, where the children sing hymns and listen to prayers and Bible readings, and the school proper, where the children are separated into classes similar to the public school classes. The teachers—adults who have volunteered for the job—consider that the main point of the class period is to tell the children a Bible story or other moral anecdote. Much of the class time is also spent on coloring religious pictures or otherwise illustrating the lessons.

During our year of observation, the various classes were crowded together in a relatively small space, and the teachers had a problem keeping order. Most of them were considerably less efficient than public school teachers in maintaining order, but this was at least partly because they were more restricted in their disciplinary measures. Since Sunday School is not compulsory or universally attended, an offended child can try to persuade his parents to take him to another Protestant Sunday School in one of the nearby communities or to let him drop it completely. The teachers have to tread a narrow line between maintaining enough semblance of order to conduct their lessons and chasing away their pupils by disciplinary measures. Each year a few children drop out or shift Sunday Schools because they have been offended by a teacher.

The elementary schoolchildren show interest in some features of Sunday School, especially in singing certain well-known rhythmic hymns, such as "The Old Rugged Cross," and in drawing and coloring. However, older children, especially boys, rapidly lose interest; most have dropped out by the age of 11.

HOLIDAYS

The regular daily routine is also altered by certain holidays which receive special attention from teachers and parents and by short vacations from school. The children are aware of most of these holidays before entering school but acquire an increasing interest in them in school.

The first major special day affecting children in the school year is Halloween. This used to be an occasion for adult toleration of childish pranks, but by the year of our study Halloween was very dull. A few store windows and house windows were soaped or waxed, but we noticed no other pranks. According to one father, "trick-or-treat" started in Orchard Town about 1950. Before then children just played tricks and did not beg for candy or other refreshments. At present they dress up in costumes and go around ringing doorbells and collecting food. Some parents organized a group of children to go around and ask for contributions to the Children's Relief Fund, feeling that it was a waste of children's time and parents' money for children to beg for candy, and that helping to buy milk for needy children in other parts of the world was a more worthy activity. One girl, aged 8, commented on this: "Ah, them poor kids, do we have to do this for them every year?" It is too early to say whether this one experience in collecting will become an established custom of Halloween, as some adults hope and expect.

The next major holiday affecting children is Thanksgiving. This is an occasion for a family gathering. If there are any grandparents or uncles and aunts living within a convenient distance, a joint family dinner is usually held. There is a large meal with a traditional menu: roast turkey, cranberries, pudding, squash, and mincemeat pie, and so on. Thanksgiving is a fairly pleasurable occasion for children, for they are often the object of attention of older visiting relatives.

At Christmas time, parties are given at church and at school. The mothers of the children supply quantities of cookies and similar items, to ensure a good Christmas party. Children imitate the custom of adults by sending greeting cards to their friends. They sometimes make a few Christmas cards in school as part of their art work. On Christmas Eve about seven children from the church went around singing Christmas Carols during our field period.

New Year's Eve is not a children's ceremony, but the practice of making New Year's resolutions is known and indulged in mostly by children, although not taken very seriously.

The major children's holiday in February is Valentine's Day. No day off from school is given for this day, but it is an occasion for special art work and the exchange of valentine greeting cards in school. Most children give a valentine to friends in their classroom and neighborhood. Comments of a teasing nature begin to be made at this time about giving valentines to a child of the opposite sex.

Of the patriotic holidays in the school year, the most important for children is Memorial Day, when there are parades by veterans' groups and family visits to the cemetery to put flowers on the graves of deceased relatives.

Easter is an important holiday although again it does not involve vacation from school. On Easter Sunday most families attend church even if they do not regularly attend the ordinary Sunday services. All of the children have new clothing for this occasion.

There is one major holiday during the summer vacation, namely, the Fourth of July or Independence Day. A generation or more ago this was, like Halloween, an occasion for tolerated pranks by children. One popular prank for older children and adolescents used to be ringing the church bell. However, long-time residents say that the Fourth is nothing like it used to be. Firecrackers are not permitted legally, and few are shot off, although there are licensed displays of fireworks in the evening in nearby towns to which some parents take their children.

RELATIONSHIP TO MOTHER

On entry into elementary school, the family relationships of the child change most with respect to the mother. Since the children can do more for themselves and are absent in school much of the time, the mother becomes less important and does less for the child. Some children seem to become more critical of their parents, especially their mothers, at this time, perhaps because they accept their teacher as a "wiser" authority.

Parents simultaneously feel that the children are less lovable once they are out of the preschool age. This is not to say, of course, that parents stop liking their children once they enter school, but they do become more reserved in their expression of affection to them. This decrease in open expression of affection is, moreover, a gradual process, not a sudden and dramatic event, and during the first two grades of school especially, there is much carry-over of the warm relationship of the mother to the preschool child.

SUMMARY

We may summarize the elementary school period briefly as involving the following developments:

1. The child becomes increasingly self-reliant.
2. He is initiated into "work" at school, although at home he continues to contribute little toward performance of household chores.
3. The prestige of both his teacher and his peers waxes while the prestige of his parents, and especially his mother, wanes somewhat.
4. Play groups split by sex, and there is an accompanying behavioral differentiation. The children express considerable aversion for the behavior of the opposite sex.
5. Children have an opportunity in school to compare themselves with a large number of peers with respect to certain standards set up by teachers, parents, and peers. They have already been motivated to make such comparisons before entering school but now have constant occasion to do so.
6. Children have their aggressive tendencies fairly well controlled and become more sociable and start to "make friends" on a larger scale than before.

Chapter 17

Later Childhood: Third through Sixth Grades

During the year of our residence in Orchard Town, children attending the third to sixth grades were marked off as a group by attending the local village schools rather than a centralized town school. This was regarded as a temporary arrangement, which would eventually be stopped when a centralized school for children from all of the component villages had been constructed. However, this grouping of the grades seems useful to us as a device for marking the later stage of childhood, a period which in any case has a certain unity and meaning for the people of Orchard Town apart from this accident of school attendance. Moreover, the break between second and third grades at the beginning of this period did not begin with the recent establishment of the centralized primary school. Previously, for many years, up into the childhood of some students in high school at the time of our study, first and second grades were combined and taught by a single teacher (as were the third and fourth, fifth, and sixth), due to the small size of the classes. However, during the year of our study, the average class size of the elementary grades was around 30, and all grades were taught separately.

The period of third to sixth grades is in many respects similar to first and second grades, and many remarks made in the previous chapter apply with little change to children in the third to sixth grades. We note below mainly the major differences between the two periods.

During our year of study, paradoxically, many older children were under a little less pressure to get up promptly in the morning than the first and second graders. This is because most of the older children lived near enough to the local village school to walk or ride their bicycles if they missed the school bus. The school bus was, nevertheless, well patronized, especially in cold or bad weather, even by children who lived within a few blocks of the school.

RIDING TO SCHOOL ON BICYCLES

Being able to ride a bicycle to school is one of the big distinguishing marks of late childhood. No first or second graders were allowed to do this during the period of study, although probably some were permitted to do so in earlier years when these grades were in the nearby village schools.

Freedom in riding a bicycle to school coincides with a general increased freedom to visit friends in others parts of town or to go out into the countryside. Children might receive their two-wheelers in first or second grade but would initially be restricted to riding them around the neighborhood.

SCHOOL SCHEDULE

The school schedule for third to sixth grade is similar to that of the first two grades. The following fourth grade schedule will serve as an example:

8:30— 8:40	Opening exercises
8:40— 9:10	Reading group A
9:10— 9:40	Reading group B
9:40—10:00	Reading group C
10:00—10:20	Recess
10:20—11:45	Arithmetic
11:45—12:30	Lunch and noon recess
12:30—12:50	Spelling
12:50— 1:25	Language (English)
1:25— 2:00	Social studies
2:00— 2:15	Music, drawing, penmanship, etc.

Lunchtime presents a different routine in the lower grades. In the small local schools there is no cafeteria. Most children bring sandwiches and eat at school in the classroom with the teacher. If they live near enough, they are free to go home for lunch, but only a few do this regularly. It is our impression that most children prefer to eat lunch at school with their classmates. Those children who stay at school eat their lunch quickly and go out to play games with their class for the rest of the noon recess.

As was mentioned in the previous chapter, the older children normally spend their recess periods in organized games. Some of these games they learn from their regular teacher or from the gym teacher, who visits them an hour every other week. Often the class chooses which game they want to play in a short discussion and vote led by the teacher. Formally organized games also become more important in children's play outside of school at this age, although since the play groups continue to be rather small, games involving sizable teams are played mostly in school or under adult supervision of some sort.

TEACHING TECHNIQUES

The formal schedule of subjects changes little from second to higher grades, but the teachers feel free to demand more of the pupils. In the first two grades, the children have presumably adjusted to the school routine, and it is now possible to demand more concentrated effort from them. Special indulgences, such as parties to celebrate holidays, decline in importance although they do not vanish. The supply of materials to occupy the time of pupils who finish their lessons rapidly now consists mostly of books to read. Standards of order and quiet in the classroom are stricter. Teachers in these grades occasionally kept unruly children after school and had them copy over appropriate moral sentences on the board. Another similar punishment was to keep the child inside at recess.

Teachers from third grade on are less indulgent toward their pupils' desire to monopolize class time by "showing off" their knowledge or abilities. The desire to "show off" remains, as evidenced by the frantic hand waving of many children when the teacher asks a question or asks for volunteers for some classroom chore, but teachers insist with greater effect that answers should not be given out of order and provide little time for children to tell about their fantasies or personal experiences not directly connected with the lesson. Teachers from fourth grade on sometimes express minor annoyance at too much hand waving, even for "legitimate" purposes, such as volunteering an answer.

Teachers give evidence of the increased importance of peer pressures by consciously manipulating the class sentiment to compel the desired behavior in unruly pupils and also sometimes by themselves taking a child-peer role in maintaining discipline. One teacher was said to make the children do "Consequences" as a punishment, for example, to get up in class and sing a song or say a poem. Another teacher was said to confiscate marbles which students showed in the classroom and make the owner win them back from her.

Training in the proper care and maintainance of property is important in the school, as in most families. A fourth grade teacher, for instance, placed considerable emphasis on the shining of shoes, and both parents and children commented favorably on this. Another way in which the school helps to encourage respect for the care of property is by having the children themselves help to buy the playground equipment, such as soccer balls, baseballs, and bats. This is done through an annual seed sale. Children volunteer to take packages of seeds and sell them from door to door throughout the town, and profits from this sale of seeds helped to pay for the playground equipment. Evidently the sum attained is not sufficient to pay a very large proportion of the actual cost for the equipment, but such behavior is felt desirable as a training device.

PARENTAL ATTITUDE TOWARD ACHIEVEMENT

Most parents expect their children to meet certain minimum standards of scholastic achievement, although they try to adjust these to what they consider the child's abilities. A good standard is one which is capable of being reached by the child with some effort. Some remarks which illustrate this include:

I think he does well enough for his age.
I know he could do better.
You can't expect a young one to do things as well as an adult would.

It is felt that a child who is not very intelligent may be made too nervous by pushing him beyond his ability. If the child becomes nervous, even otherwise possible goals cannot be reached.

One mother tells how she changed her techniques on discovering that her daughter had a low "potential."

When I first saw she wasn't doing well in reading, I was quite cross. This made her very nervous. Then I realized she didn't have much memory span and I tried to have patience with her, and I would say, "Now I know you don't know, but let's try to find out."

Although she lowered her intellectual standards, this same mother felt it was unnecessary to change another goal: "You may not be able to get A's in reading and arithmetic, but you can get an A in conduct."

But parents are often slow to admit that their child's ability is low. Other reasons are sought, reasons that may indeed be the basis of the child's lack of success. The reason for failure that produces the greatest anger and punishment from parents is the feeling that the child is not trying. It may even be that the parent feels that the child wishes to be an embarrassing representative of the parent—to get even with the parent in some way. One parent reports about such a child:

> He could do better than he does (in school) if he could learn to mind his own business a little more. We get disgusted because he's capable. He's no genius, but he could do better than he does. . . . Well, we've worked at home with him on it. Mostly it's a case, if he just paid attention, his marks would come up. We took his bike away after the first marking period until the second set of marks came out. . . . I'd get so impatient working with him here at home that I'd do more harm than good because sometimes he'd do it and other times he would just fool around.

In one child, several of the factors which might cause conflict in the realm of achievement behavior were combined. The child was a member of a highly upwardly mobile family whose mother and father had risen considerably in status. One received a strong impression that the child was regarded as a representative of the parents but also that the child was hostile to the parents. Here is what the mother says about her dissatisfaction with the child's work:

> Well, I'm afraid I'm not very satisfied. She doesn't get all A's in school. She doesn't perform her tasks to perfection. She's inclined to be a little lazy. The only thing she really does well is something that captures her interest. . . . Her room is always carelessly done. She leaves things setting if I don't put them over the sink [when she does dishes]. She usually shoves the dishpan under the counter wet. Sometimes she has to do things over two or three times before she does them right.

Parents feel that it is more important for boys to "do well" than it is for girls, since a girl may gain status and popularity through personal beauty. Mothers say:

> I feel that my son is more important than my daughters. So we spend much more time on his education.
> I don't feel my girls will ever be any great shakes anyway. They'll probably get married.

For a girl, her achievement will generally be measured in terms of that of her husband.

CHORES

In later childhood parents demand a little more from their children in tasks and errands around the house, but these demands are not great. Children are expected to keep their rooms orderly when reminded. They are also often expected to help wash dishes. Delaying actions are not uncommon according to both observations and mothers' reports. The following mother's report will serve as an example of the chores of a 10-year-old boy and his performance of them.

> In the morning he is supposed to get up, shove the heat up and put the dogs out; and almost always I have to call down and almost always one or the other or both haven't been done. This morning I called down about the heat and later I called again, and he said, "You told me about that before," and I said, "Yes, but did you take care of it?" I heard him go over and turn the heat up, and then he said, "Yes."

Some parents pay their children small sums for doing work at home, but other parents do not, often on the ground that child-training experts oppose it, for payment would prevent the children from feeling their responsibilities as family members. Still others have tried payments but later abandoned them as an ineffective incentive for consistent performance, at least payments of the size the parents are willing to offer.

Perhaps one reason why parents demand so little work from the children around the house is because they hope for so much from them in their schoolwork and in other forms of competition with their peers.

AFTER SCHOOL ACTIVITIES

After-school activities are in many ways similar to those of elementary schoolchildren. Indeed, in neighborhood play groups there is no sharp boundary between the two age groups. The third to sixth graders, however, have more freedom as to the area in which they may play. If they have a little pocket money, they are free to go to a store to buy gum, candy, inexpensive toys, and so on. In good weather boys of this age may tramp through the surrounding woods and fields, collecting birds' eggs, fishing, swimming in shallow ponds (perhaps without parental knowledge), and so forth.

Boys would like BB guns and 22-caliber rifles which would really shoot, but police regulations prevent this and are enforced. Most parents also would probably be hesitant about giving their sons such weapons. Many boys, however, look forward to the time when they will be old enough to own a 22 or a more powerful weapon and hunt with these.

ORGANIZED ACTIVITIES

Also, from third grade on the children become increasingly involved in various organized activities. These include the "Scouts," the church junior choir (third grade up), baseball teams, dancing classes, and so on.

Scouts are important for most boys and girls but are perhaps thought of as more educational than recreational. Scouts and the adult leaders take themselves quite seriously at times. One adult leader said in a speech at a troop dinner, "Our requirements are not easy, but one cannot learn to survive in the forest by performing simple tasks."

Scouts are divided into two major age grades, in addition to having these groups further divided according to many achieved statuses. The younger children are "Brownies" or "Cub Scouts" while the older children are in Boy or Girl Scouts proper.

There have been Boy Scouts in Orchard Town for a generation or so, but the Girl Scouts are more recent. Scouts are active during both the school year and the vacation. The Girl Scouts have a day camp during vacation where the girls spend most of their time in organized games and activities.

Most children from the religiously active families participate in the junior choir from third through fifth grades. There are a few children in the junior choir after the fifth grade also. The junior choir has an evening rehearsal once a week and sings occasionally at the Sunday morning services and also on special occasions, such as Christmas, Easter, and at special gatherings of children's choirs of other churches.

The children's baseball teams are known as the "Minor League" (for boys from about fifth grade) and the "Little League" (for somewhat older boys). Each team is sponsored by a local business firm or fraternal association. Boys must try out to become eligible. The adult coach and supervisors provide regular attention, although the interest of many parents is rather perfunctory. At one Minor League game which one of us attended, the spectators numbered a couple of dozen, scarcely more than the number of players.

In the summer during vacation time there have been organized swimming classes sponsored by the Red Cross in a nearby town. Also there have been classes at a Y.M.C.A. in a nearby town.

The dancing classes are another instance of organized recreation and education outside of school. Children begin attending at the age of about 10. During the year of our study there were two dancing classes in town: a square dancing class sponsored by the North Village Woman's Club and a ballroom dancing class sponsored by the Center Club. This caused some confusion, for the boys preferred the square dancing class and the girls preferred the ballroom dancing class.

The dancing classes were interesting from the point of view of teaching social etiquette in groups. The teacher demonstrates the social graces as well as the dancing. He instructs the children to "go right up and make yourself known." He tries to be amusing to impress the children and to keep their attention. The following excerpt is taken from an observation of the dancing group.

You are not boys and girls, because in this class you are ladies and gentlemen. I don't think I have to refer to each individual as far as conduct is concerned. I refer to you as a group. It's not just the class, it's (conduct) important in everyday life." "Now, when you sit down, gentlemen, you don't sit down like this [demonstrates sloppy sitting]; you sit down in one piece. Girls generally do not cross the knees, but gentlemen may cross their knees this way. There's a place for your feet—it's not on the furniture, of course. I'd like to see the gentlemen stand up and sit down in one piece. What about the fellow on the end there? He's tired before he starts. Now the girls."

"Gentlemen, stand up and walk across the hall and ask a girl to be your partner. [Boys got up and rushed across to get their favorite girls.] You'd think this was a track meet! You go and ask Alberta and she says, "Thank you." Gentlemen, will you kindly take your partner back to her seats and thank her again for the dance. Let's go to your seats walking.

During the dance the teacher was careful to see that all the girls had male partners at one time or another, and he did his best to see that none of the children were wallflowers.

INTEREST IN THE OPPOSITE SEX

The existence of the dancing school for children around the age of 10 is symptomatic of an increasing interest in the opposite sex on the part of both boys and girls, after the earlier period of strong antipathy in first and second grades. This heterosexual interest develops progressively in late childhood, although individual children differed considerably in the age at which they began to manifest an interest. According to a woman who gave lectures to Sunday School teachers throughout the area, there was also considerable variation between communities in the average age at which boys and girls began to take an interest in each other. By fourth grade some of the boys would admit with embarrassment that they had a "girl friend," although, as far as we could see, these relationships consisted mainly of secret admiration and overt teasing, and the couple saw little of each other outside of school.

By fifth grade some of the couples were playing together at times after school, usually in larger groups. We heard of one fifth grader who had wanted to take his "girl" to an afternoon movie show. His mother discouraged this, however. Judging from a small amount of observation of one fifth grade couple in a play group, teasing was still prominent in the relationship, but "serious" talk and play could also take place.

MODESTY

A sense of modesty about exposure of the unclothed body grows stronger in late childhood, although simple knowledge of the rules of modesty exists before this. One mother reported a rumor of an incident at school where a group of 9- or 10-year-old boys and girls dared one girl to pull up her dress. But supposedly this was in cold weather when she was wearing trousers under the dress. One 9-year-old who had the reputation of being rather uninhibited told of an incident where he had been swimming in a pond in his underpants and had had to hide behind some brush on an island so some girls who came by would not see him. A child of this age who was openly exhibitionistic would be disapproved of as being "dirty."

It is unclear to us how much sexual knowledge these children have. They at least have the idea of some sort of attraction between a boy and a girl. They also have the idea that there are activities about which it is inappropriate to speak. On one occasion one of us listened to some jokes which some 10-year-olds considered "dirty." However, these jokes were mostly about elimination or involved words which were considered blasphemous, such as "Hell." One joke involved a misinterpretation of the function of brassieres. There were no jokes which involved sexual intercourse. It is hard to say what is meant by a 10-year-old who says to his friend, "You learned a lot from her, eh?"

Children are not supposed to use bad language, which includes both obscene language and certain forms of blasphemy. One incident was reported where a boy called something "cock-eyed penis," and his mother hit him in the mouth and "it shocked him." Another mother reported washing her daughter's mouth out with soap for "bad language." Just what this was was unspecified. It may have involved the daughter talking back to her as well as obscenity, if it involved obscenity at all.

Kissing is a subject of joking, especially with children from 9 or so on. It is also a subject of horseplay. One incident was reported where some 11-year-old girls were trying to catch a 10-year-old boy to kiss him. The boy was supposedly trying to escape them because his own girl friend was not involved. At this age girls may show some initiative in joking or horseplay, but a few years later such joking or horseplay would not be approved of and would be rare if it occurred at all. Some young girls, who were playing "Truth or Consequences," were observed joking among themselves about sexual subjects and asking each other such questions as "Would you like to kiss so-and-so?" or "Would you like to go in the tunnel of love with him?" or "Do you like such-and-such a boy?" The questioned girl would sometimes try to deny this, but then she would be made to do something as a payment of consequences for saying something unbelievable.

SEX ROLE

The resumption of interest, in late childhood, in persons of the opposite sex suggests that the first two grades of school in Orchard Town are the principal period for the establishment of what might be termed the public sex role. Once the children are confirmed in this, they can again turn their attention toward members of the opposite sex with little danger of inappropriate imitation.

However, it is true that signs of envy of the opposite sex remain, especially on the part of girls. Some girls express resentment of the greater freedom given to boys of school age, and they also may feel they have to do more work at home than boys. Perhaps in compensation for this, the rules about crossing sex-role lines are more lenient for girls than for boys. We observed some instances of a boy playing girls' games. The criticism of this by other children was more severe than criticism of girls playing boys' games or doing things which are considered primarily boys' activities. One may also note that girls sometimes wear boys' clothes, either clothes actually belonging to a male member of their family or clothes made for women, but in imitation of men's clothes, such as slacks. The reverse does not occur.

SUNDAY SCHOOL

A majority of the sample children in later childhood continued to go to Sunday School, although often with more resistance than younger children. The boys especially became increasingly disorderly with age, hitting each other on the head with hymnals and engaging in other "horseplay."

In addition to Sunday School proper, children are encouraged to attend the regular adult morning service, although only a few actually do. The minister is in the habit of giving a special children's sermon, usually a historical or biographical incident, or fable or fairytale illustrating some moral point. Children are free to leave during the hymn before the sermon begins, but older children usually remain through the entire service if they come at all.

Most children who attend Sunday School regularly do so because their parents insist on it. However, the Sunday School authorities try to arouse the children's interest in various ways with some success. Attendance pins were given to children who had perfect attendance records, with allowance made for legitimate excuses. The use of the attendance pin as an incentive for coming to Sunday School, however, has been abandoned by a number of other nearby Protestant churches and is regarded with mixed feelings by members of the North Village church.

Certain events during the year also arouse genuine interest in the children. Of these the most important is probably the Christmas party. Some children are suspected of attending Sunday School several Sundays before Christmas in order to justify their appearance at the Christmas party and then stopping for the rest of the year. The year of our study, the Christmas party consisted of a movie and ice cream for the children, followed by the appearance of Santa Claus handing out presents. Children's Sunday, which occurred at the end of the Sunday School year in June, is another occasion which interests the children. On this occasion certificates of graduation are given to the children; attendance awards are given; children finishing the third grade are given a Bible, and every child receives a small potted plant. No special significance is given for this plant.

SUMMARY

To summarize the developments of the children in later childhood, there are:

1. Growing independence from the parents, although partly by a transfer of dependence to the teacher.
2. Increased parental and school demands for personal achievement or success but less indulgence of "showing off."

3. More formal organization of activity, even of play with peers, which often consists of formal games.

4. Growing pressure from one's own agemates to conform to the current fashions and growing sensitivity to this pressure.

5. Effective control of aggressive tendencies. Serious physical fighting is rare, almost entirely between boys, and even in the heat of anger is usually controlled enough to prevent serious injury.

6. Growing attraction between the sexes.

✻
✻
✻

Epilogue

Orchard Town: an Overview

What is the general significance of this study of Orchard Town? To a considerable extent the significance of a book is what its readers make of it: in this sense, a book is not finished when it is written. We can, of course, give some idea of what the significance of Orchard Town was and was not for us personally and scientifically. We did not pick Orchard Town as an ideal or typical American community, and we do not now maintain that it is especially representative. We did try to select a community which seemed reasonably homogeneous, socially and ethnically, and which lacked serious social problems, and we believe that we succeeded in this. But Orchard Town is hardly representative of the region, let alone the nation. It is surrounded by other communities, many of which might also have been suitable for our study, but each of which would have been different in some significant way, smaller or larger, richer or poorer, more and less socially stratified, etc.

Our concern in selecting a community for study was primarily to have a unit with some degree of stability in which most of the activities of child rearing would take place, and which would therefore be comparable to the communities studied in other cultures in the Six Cultures project. As such, we were not concerned with representativeness. At one point, for example, we were considering choosing a long-established fishing community settled by English Catholics from the Channel Islands; this could hardly have been considered a typical community. However, our preference for Orchard Town was not based on its being more typical than this fishing community, but simply on the fact that Orchard Town appeared to us to be at the time a more integrated community with less serious socioeconomic problems than the fishing group. Of course, we must admit that perhaps one reason why Orchard Town had less serious problems is that it was more typical of the larger society.

Our report on Orchard Town was written specifically for comparison with the reports of the other five cultures studied by our colleagues, and it may be most profitable to the reader to examine our study along with one or more of the others. We hope, however, that it has value in itself as well, but this value will depend on what the reader is seeking. Presumably most of the readers will be Americans. Those reading the report for regional curiosa will be disappointed; there are regional touches here and there in the report and we could have added more, but it was our intention to describe the general outlines of contemporary life in the town. To the extent that these outlines coincide with the outlines of life elsewhere in the United States, the American reader will simply be encountering something quite familiar.

Those reading the report for identification of major problems may also be disappointed. The work is not intended as social criticism. We did not attempt to reform Orchard Town or its people; we simply wished to describe the major features of life there, good and bad, as we saw them in rather universalistic terms. We have included little evaluation, except for the evaluation provided by the people themselves.

The study may be of some value in comparison with other studies of American communities by other writers. Although we did not construct our report primarily for this purpose, we have lived in various parts of the country, and we also had some familiarity with the literature on American communities before we began our fieldwork. Therefore, some of the facts were recorded undoubtedly because of the contrast they provide with some other part of the country, although we did not do this systematically. Moreover, we believe that most of our American readers, whatever motivates them to pick up the book, are likely to have a similar interest in comparing Orchard Town with other American communities they have known. Thus we would like to comment on the significance of this interest for Americans and give a very impressionistic evaluation of the position of Orchard Town in American society and culture.

SELF-CRITICISM AND THE FEMININE CONSCIENCE

If you are an American, the literature on American culture and character is often depressing reading. Partly, this is because many of the studies are written by psychiatrists who daily encounter pathologies arising out of our particular system of socialization, or by social critics who wish to point out how we might improve ourselves. But this is not the only ،reason for such a response. Most important is what Margaret Mead notes as the typical American's dissatisfaction with his particular family and childhood. Each of us has his own version of how he failed to receive satisfactory treatment in his childhood household, and it is in the very nature of American culture that we should convince ourselves of the justice of our dissatisfactions (Mead, 1949, p. 255). Accordingly, when we read the literature on American society and culture, we inevitably compare what we know through firsthand experience with the views of the author.

What can we say then, by way of apology, to the mothers of Orchard Town, some of whom consented quite graciously to provide the data for this book, a book upon which all of us can now project the dissatisfactions of our own childhoods and parenthoods? American culture in many ways offers Orchard Town mothers a changing and vague formula for how to behave as parents. To paraphrase Parsons (1964, p. 161), each of us is given the task, not simply to succeed in terms set forth by the culture, but to evaluate the cultural terms of success and the limits of his rights and obligations in it.

It is supposed to be possible to be the perfect parent in America. But presumably the perfect parent will differ, depending upon the kind of adult one wishes to create. What kind of person, indeed, is desirable in a changing world? Each of the mothers of Orchard Town has made her own guess at what kind would be best, with concern for her child uppermost in her mind. Where the behavior of Orchard Town mothers does not live up to their own ideals or grand designs, they are the first to blame themselves. Their desire to understand the whole business of motherhood better was perhaps their primary motivation in consenting to contribute to the study.

The matter of blaming one's mother is an important aspect of American life and child training. Some of the reasons for this habit show up clearly in Orchard Town observations. Analysis of interviews with these mothers shows that in comparison with the mothers of the other five cultures studied, the New England mothers are "significantly higher than any other group on the proportion of time they are in charge of babies. . . ." (Minturn and Lambert, 1964, pp. 191–192). No wonder that, as Mead has said, the voice of conscience is feminine (Mead, 1949, p. 312) and the problem of "Momism" is peculiarly American. Who else does the American child have to identify with, project upon, and internalize as a superego?

Erikson, who is somewhat sympathetic to American "Moms," observes one of the pathologies of our system in patients who fail to get support unless they behave (Erikson, 1950, p. 247), and Mead too sees us giving up our freedom for parental support (1949, p. 278). Orchard Town belies this somewhat. The idea is rather firmly implanted in most Orchard Town mothers' minds that children should be expected to behave only within certain limits. Sometimes these are internal limits within the child's own nature, which the mother must divine or can never quite know; at other times they are cultural limits which announce that boys may be expected to misbehave in certain ways. To support this point, Minturn and Lambert (1964, p. 195) find that "Orchard Town mothers rank fifth [out of six cultures studied] in both consistency of obedience training and expectation of prompt obedience, and are significantly lower than most other societies on both these scales." Furthermore, support is not consistently withdrawn for these behavioral infractions.

The idea that American child training involves approval conditional upon success needs examination in more depth. Indeed, in Orchard Town, happiness is often preferred to success for one's children. For some mothers happiness is inconceivable without success, it is true; for others success would be nice, but it is not expected or considered necessary. American values may be changing in this regard. One has only to read the congratulations of the newspaper columnist Ann Landers to women who have good husbands and good children but little money or status to realize that there is more than one side to the success story of American characters. The Calvinistic philosophy of life is passing out of style, or evolving.

One reason why mothers are blamed for the unhappiness of their children is discussed in Chapter 11, The Nature of the Child in Orchard Town. Mothers are expected to use all the means at their command to discover the hidden guide to the development of the ideal potential of each child which lies buried in the child's nature. Insofar as none of us is perfect, we can always attribute our imperfections to our mothers' failure to find the correct way to our ideal development, or to their distortion of the path to render it congenial to their own images. Guilt is built into this system, and the sins of the mothers are visited upon the children.

However, the mother's guilt is supposed to be limited to our childhood years. When we become adults and if we have internalized the values, it is then up to us to correct our mother's mistakes and realize our own potentials. In other words, we become responsible for our own failure to achieve success or happiness. Depression follows when we fail to do so. In this state of mind, blaming "Mom" can become a useful defense. On the other hand, blaming "Mom" can also keep us trying to achieve some ideal state—working on the problem ourselves and showing up her errors. If we were really failures, we might as well give up.

WHAT MAKES US AMERICANS

Although the fact that we are trained almost exclusively by our mothers in our preschool years is perhaps one of the most important elements in shaping American character, there are other things which give American character its particular slant. It is difficult to put causative labels on these factors, identifying them as historical, cultural, sociological, or environmental in nature, since the facts crosscut these categories. It is easier, instead, to say that some things are very important in the development of American character and to let the reader invent labels of his own if he wishes.

In discussing factors thought to be important in the development of American character, we will begin with some of the findings of the Six Cultures study and then proceed to some points noted by other authors. Following each observation, an attempt will be made to place Orchard Town in the general American context.

In analyzing the interviews of mothers in six cultures, Minturn and Lambert (1964, pp. 189–199) find that, compared to the mothers in the African, Mexican, Indian, Philippine, and Okinawan communities studied, Orchard Town mothers are not remarkable in relation to the following variables: warmth of mother, hostility of mother, amount of praise used in child training, and emotional stability of mothers. However, in this sample of six cultures the American mothers vary significantly in certain areas. They report using less physical punishment than mothers in any of the other cultures (see also Miller and Swanson, 1958, p. 13, for a discussion of the disappearance of physical punishment in American culture from the historical point of view. They also expect less prompt obedience than mothers in four of the cultures, and children are assigned fewer chores other than house-cleaning, which they are said to do more often than the children in the other cultures. Most important of all, perhaps, Orchard Town children are encouraged to retaliate for aggression from their peers, in great contrast to the other groups. Within the New England group, mothers are much less strong in their punishment for aggression to peers than they are in punishment for aggression directed toward themselves. Furthermore, they have the least consistency among the six cultures about rules for aggression. Fighting fairly, however, is learned early. The English value of "fair play" expounded by Salvador de Madariaga (1931) is also, to a great extent, an Orchard Town value.

It is easy to imagine that this combination of factors might create an adult who is prone to respond more to principles handed down from authorities and less to the need for cooperation in joint ventures with peers. Extremes of this tendency are balanced by some factors not accounted for in this story of Orchard Town children; the study does not take into consideration their adolescence when positive peer relations are strengthened. However, the foundations of *individual* productivity, creativity, and isolation are laid down early in life in Orchard Town.

The Six Cultures study was designed to discover significant differences both within and between cultures. Minturn and Lambert report that the study was a success in both respects. Accordingly, the parents of Orchard Town are not altogether unique in showing appreciable variations in their ways of bringing up their children. Both Mead and Kardiner have emphasized behavioral variability as importantly American, but they interpret differently the meaning of this phenomenon. Mead thinks that the very universality of special "family codes" paradoxically shows our essential likeness (1949, p. 251). Kardiner, on the other hand, recognizes much heterogeneity but emphasizes that differences exist especially in matters of detail, not in essential institutions such as monogamy, or in the consequent basic personality structure. According to Kardiner, rapid social change makes American social institutions more difficult for the social scientist to grasp, but this social change tends to be adaptive; tendencies toward increased diversity are thus limited (Kardiner, 1945, pp. 339–340). Since Kardiner derives his idea of basic personality structure from what he calls "primary institutions," and considers that American primary institutions are hardly more variable than those of simpler societies, he feels that American basic personality structure has enough stability to warrant investigation.

Our selection of Orchard Town as the unit of our study set limits on the variations we would encounter in child-training patterns. Within this unit we further limited the variability by selecting normal children for study. These were children from intact families. Most of the sample families were wholly Protestant in their religious backgrounds, although in a few cases Catholicism occurred on one side of the family or in past generations. Even under these controlled conditions significant variations with the group on child training remain, but the total variation in American culture cannot be understood from this sample alone.

One gets the impression, after reading the historical account of child-rearing practices in America in Miller and Swanson (1958, pp. 3–63), that most of the child-rearing themes gaining ascendancy in the popular literature can still be found as practices in segments of a community like Orchard Town. One or another of these practices will be considered correct, depending upon whom you are talking to. In the account of Orchard Town these variations are seen as different means to the same end—they guide the child in expressing his potential.

Both Potter (1954) and Erikson (1950) have remarked on the importance of the frontier in the formation of American character. The idea that American individualism, dislike of controls, regard for equality of opportunity, optimism, and practicality, among other things, can be traced to the existence of the frontier through a long period of our history, was considered in greatest detail by Turner (1920). Erikson (1950, p. 252) points out the difficulties faced by mothers who had to prepare children for the eventualities both of remaining at home and of attacking life directly on the frontier. America must certainly have beckoned selectively to the more adventurous spirits of Europe—to those who perhaps were more rebellious in nature. To create a stable nation, some of this rebelliousness had to be bred out of the frontier children. Erikson's ideas are applicable in many ways in modern Orchard Town. In his view, the lure of the frontier forced those who remained behind to become "defensively proud" of their settled way of life. The phrase *defensively proud* sums up in a remarkable way the stereotyped view of New England character that existed at least until recently in the rest of America. The Old-Timers of Orchard Town still gave this impression to the Newcomers in 1954. "Our way is good enough." "You are not one of us." "We don't need the help of anyone." "Look how much worse off those others are than I am." These sentiments are either heard from the Old-Timers or put into their mouths by the Newcomers. The old New Englanders, after all, were those who stayed behind in the later phases of the conquest of the frontier.

The present situation in Orchard Town is complex in terms of the sedentary life versus the adventure of the frontier. The modern city, with its varied opportunities, its social fluidity and disorder, is in some sense a kind of frontier. To the city dweller, moving to Orchard Town represents a return to settled community life. The former city dweller becomes the Newcomer. He wants to escape the restrictions and disorder of city life. The Newcomers are those who not so long ago represented a way of life against which the Old-Timers have long been defensively proud. These people, like James West's farmers in Plainville, felt inferior when they compared themselves to city folk.

However, every Orchard Towner, Old-Timer or Newcomer, has to prepare his children to face the unknown. Orchard Town is almost completely lacking in young unmarried people; most of the children go away to college or into the city for a job when they reach the proper age. There will be very little continuity between the new and the old generations of Orchard Town. Unlike Plainville there are no longer any farms for eldest sons to take over, and very little enterprise of a family nature for some to inherit. Children must be trained to make their own way and choose work in line with their inner nature.

In this sense the frontier has returned even to Orchard Town with the decline of local agriculture. But in another sense, people move to Orchard Town with some hope of identifying with the historical roots of the place—to feel as though they belong in a continuing sense to a group. Recent developments in Orchard Town, as it becomes increasingly populated with city people seeking the sedentary life, indicate this feeling; an anecdote in a letter from an Orchard Town mother written in 1964 serves as an illustration.

Thought you might be interested in a new development in Orchard Town— a historical consciousness. We now have a Historical Society about two years old, a Chairman of Public Celebrations, and a Patriots' Day Committee. The local D.A.R. has come to life, too. The most interesting part of it all is that these activities have been initiated and carried out by people from Ohio, Texas, etc.—all outlanders! My husband and I went to a dinner party Saturday night and I saw the Chairman in action . . . telling people that they had "certainly done their share to put Orchard Town into the history books of this country. . . ." Of course, it *was* nine o'clock and we were still working on cocktails. But this the general tone of the whole thing.

People actually crawl out of bed at about 6:00 A.M. two days in a row for these festivities. . . . And a goodly number walk . . . through the woods by the same path the Minute Men took. Pressure has been put on the owners of the land to sign easements to the town for this route, and a number of sections have already been 'eased' in this way so that people can make this pilgrimage at any time of the year. I would like to go along some time and see whether this group includes any old residents or is made up mostly of newcomers. Everything—music, costumes, etc.—is authentic. Most of the men at the

Patriots' Day Ball are paunchy and middle-aged, but, as I told my husband, probably the real revolutionaries looked much the same.

David Potter (1954) has chosen to emphasize *abundance* as the important element in child training that leads to an American character. Orchard Town shares to some extent in all the training factors which Potter says are results of abundance. These factors include feeding of bottled milk, wearing of light clothing because of central heating, permissive toilet training with the advent of washing machines and paper diapers, living and young parents, freedom from agricultural labor for children, more leisure time for fathers to spend with children, mothers rather than nurses as full-time attendants for children, contact with a peer group outside of parental control rather than with siblings only, late age of economic responsibility and earlier age of sexual associations.

There is variation in Orchard Town on most of these points, however. Most of Potter's points are evidently intended to compare American to European child training, and to compare recent with past American practices. As members of a Northern semirural community, Orchard Town children perhaps wear warmer clothing than children in many parts of America. Some fathers have considerably less leisure time than many city fathers have to spend with their children. Fathers who commute to the city for work have to spend long hours away from home. In addition, a number of fathers in Orchard Town have occupations which keep them away from home overnight many times a week.

Religion and political ideology cannot be neglected as part of the foundation of American character. For a long time Western man's character has been felt to be significantly influenced by the Protestant Ethic. Like James West's Plainville, Orchard Town is not excessively dominated by an extreme form of Calvinist morality. These ethics still make themselves felt in certain long-established families, but they are perhaps in the minority. A more lenient and hopeful view of human nature is common now. Of course, the idea that every individual is responsible for his own salvation continues in the form of the belief that potential must be found within the self. In the lives of many Orchard Towners religion plays a rather minor role. Even the most extreme religious groups of Plainville which gave some vitality to the religion of the lower classes in that community are missing in Orchard Town. Salvation has a powerful meaning in only a few lives.

Neither are there extremes of political ideologies. Mead (1949, pp. 259–260) identifies liberalism, centrality, and reactionism as three ways of dealing with the discrepancies between the real and the ideal in

American life. Orchard Town represents mostly centrality, although from the point of view of some other parts of the country it might be classified toward the liberal end of the continuum. The Orchard Towners consider themselves conservative compared to the liberalism of the city. Political ideology has not taken the place of religion in the lives of these people.

No discussion of American character and training can neglect mention of the importance of the machine, industrialization, and our system of distributing wealth as factors in the formation of character. Fromm (1941) has made much of this, and such changes are responsible for Riesman's alarm at our becoming other-directed (1950). Orchard Town children are, or were in 1954, affected by this rather more peripherally than many American children. Although they have their share of material possessions, they have no large sources of supply of these goods immediately within the town. Advertising reaches them via television and does not assault the landscape of the area, which is still beautiful and almost virgin compared to other American places of residence. A much more focused study would be needed to determine how the business orientation influences the lives of the children in this largely residential town. Money *is* valuable to parents and children alike, and it is not plentiful enough in Orchard Town to be considered lightly.

In our chapter on the nature of the child, we said in a different way that the core of Orchard Town values, surpassing in importance the value of service to God or the political community, is perhaps what Hsu calls *self-reliance.* If we add to self-reliance *self-realization,* the aim in the development of Orchard Town character is perhaps largely complete. Hsu (1961, p. 217) regards self-reliance as the American core value and considers that other values take on color from it. The Orchard Town belief in developing the inner potential of the child can be regarded as a manifestation of self-reliance. Talcott Parsons (1964, p. 159) calls this core value *instrumental activism.* This term is not quite the same as Hsu's self-reliance, but these concepts have many similarities. Parsons is especially interesting when he suggests that this value is at work on the societal as well as on the individual level. That is, valued achievement must take place openly in the society, and the society is considered as a sort of stage for achievement; at the same time a contribution to the progressive improvement of the society is the best kind of individual achievement (Parsons, 1965, p. 160).

We have tried to show here how Orchard Town differs from or is similar to the various conceptions about the nature and shaping of American character. In doing this we hope to establish in the mind of the reader just how typical of America this sample can be considered to be. North Village is neither a farming community, nor a city community, nor an industrial community, nor quite yet a suburb. It has its connections with all these ways of American life. It represents the New England region in many respects, and differs from the Middle Western, Western, Southern, and other towns insofar as it does. It is neither a rich nor a poor town. Its economic resources are in many ways brought in from other places where the fathers of Orchard Town go to work. In short, although it is neither an ideal microcosm of American society nor a self-contained community in its own right, Orchard Town is not especially unusual as an American community and it does have enough identity and integration to make it useful to study as a local arena of child rearing.

BIBLIOGRAPHY

Erikson, Erik H. *Childhood and Society*. New York: W. W. Norton, 1950.

Fromm, Erich. *Escape From Freedom*. New York: Farrar and Rinehart, 1941.

Hsu, Francis L. K. American Core Value and National Character. In Francis L. K. Hsu (Ed.), *Psychological Anthropology: Approaches to Culture and Personality*. Homewood, Ill.: The Dorsey Press, 1961.

Kardiner, Abram, with the collaboration of Ralph Linton, Cora De Bois and James West. *The Psychological Frontiers of Society*. New York: Columbia University Press, 1945.

de Madariaga, Salvador. *Englishmen, Frenchmen and Spaniards*. London: Oxford University Press, 1931.

Mead, Margaret. *Male and Female*. New York: William Morrow, 1949.

Miller, Daniel R., and Swanson, Guy E. *The Changing American Parent*. New York: John Wiley and Sons, 1958.

Minturn, Leigh, et al. *Mothers of Six Cultures: Antecedents of Child Rearing*. New York: John Wiley and Sons, 1964.

Parsons, Talcott. Youth in the Context of American Society. In *Social Structure and Personality*. New York: The Free Press of Glencoe, Collier-Macmillan Ltd., 1964.

Potter, David. *People of Plenty*. Chicago: The University of Chicago Press, 1954.

Riesman, David. *The Lonely Crowd*. New Haven, Conn.: Yale University Press, 1950.

Whiting, Beatrice B. (ed.). *Six Cultures: Studies of Child Rearing*. New York: John Wiley and Sons, 1963.

Whiting, John, et al. *Field Guide for a Study of Socialization in Five Societies*. Cambridge, Mass.: Laboratory of Human Development, 1954 (mimeographed).

Index